SHEPHERD'S NOTES
Christian Classics

*C.S. Lewis's
Mere Christianity*

HOLMAN
REFERENCE

NASHVILLE, TENNESSEE

Shepherd's Notes—C. S. Lewis *Mere Christianity*
© 1999
by Broadman & Holman Publishers
Nashville, Tennessee
All rights reserved
Printed in the United States of America

978–0–8054–9347–4
Dewey Decimal Classification: 230
Subject Heading: C. S. Lewis
Library of Congress Card Catalog Number: 99–37906

**Dedicated to Parker Hayden Miethe,
a true princess**

Library of Congress Cataloging-in-Publication Data
Miethe, Terry L., 1948–
    C. S. Lewis' Mere Christianity / by Terry L. Miethe.
        p. cm. — (Shepherd's notes. Christian classics)
    Includes bibliographical references.
    ISBN 0–8054–9347–6 (alk. paper)
        1. Lewis, C. S. (Clive Staples), 1898–1963. Mere Christinaity. 2. Theology
Doctrinal—Popular works. 3. Apologetics. 4. Christian ethics—Anglican authors
I. Title. II. Series.
BT77.M526   1999
230—dc21   99–3790
                                                                              CI

17 18 19 20 21 22 23   13 12 11 10 09
R

SHEPHERD'S NOTES

Shepherd's Notes Titles Available

SHEPHERD'S NOTES COMMENTARY SERIES

Old Testament

9-780-805-490-282 Genesis
9-780-805-490-565 Exodus
9-780-805-490-695 Leviticus, Numbers
9-780-805-490-275 Deuteronomy
9-780-805-490-589 Joshua, Judges
9-780-805-490-572 Ruth, Esther
9-780-805-490-633 1 & 2 Samuel
9-780-805-490-077 1 & 2 Kings
9-780-805-490-649 1 & 2 Chronicles
9-780-805-491-944 Ezra, Nehemiah
9-780-805-490-060 Job
9-780-805-493-399 Psalms 1-50

9-780-805-493-405 Psalms 51-100
9-780-805-493-412 Psalms 101-150
9-780-805-490-169 Proverbs
9-780-805-490-596 Ecclesiastes, Song of
Solomon
9-780-805-491-975 Isaiah
9-780-805-490-701 Jeremiah, Lamentations
9-780-805-490-787 Ezekiel
9-780-805-490-152 Daniel
9-780-805-493-269 Hosea, Obadiah
9-780-805-493-344 Jonah, Zephaniah
9-780-805-490-657 Haggai, Malachi

New Testament

9-781-558-196-889 Matthew
9-780-805-490-718 Mark
9-780-805-490-046 Luke
9-781-558-196-933 John
9-781-558-196-919 Acts
9-780-805-490-053 Romans
9-780-805-493-252 1 Corinthians
9-780-805-493-351 2 Corinthians
9-781-558-196-902 Galatians
9-780-805-493-276 Ephesians

9-781-558-196-896 Philippians, Colossians,
Philemon
9-780-805-490-008 1 & 2 Thessalonians
9-781-558-196-926 1 & 2 Timothy, Titus
9-780-805-493-368 Hebrews
9-780-805-490-183 James
9-780-805-490-190 1 & 2 Peter & Jude
9-780-805-492-149 1, 2 & 3 John
9-780-805-490-176 Revelation

SHEPHERD'S NOTES CHRISTIAN CLASSICS

9-780-805-493-474 *Mere Christianity,*
C. S. Lewis
9-780-805-493-535 *The Problem of Pain/*
A Grief Observed,
C. S. Lewis
9-780-805-491-999 *The Confessions,*
Augustine
9-780-805-492-002 *Calvin's Institutes*
9-780-805-493-948 *Miracles,* C. S. Lewis

9-780-805-491-968 *Lectures to My Students,*
Charles Haddon
Spurgeon
9-780-805-492-200 *The Writings of Justin*
Martyr
9-780-805-493-450 *The City of God,*
Augustine
9-780-805-491-982 *The Cost of Discipleship,*
Bonhoeffer

SHEPHERD'S NOTES — BIBLE SUMMARY SERIES

9-780-805-493-771 Old Testament
9-780-805-493-788 New Testament

9-780-805-493-849 Life & Teachings of Jesus
9-780-805-493-856 Life & Letters of Paul

CONTENTS

Dear Reader:

Shepherd's Notes—Classics Series is designed to give you a quick, step-by-step overview of some of the enduring treasures of the Christian faith. They are designed to be used alongside the classic itself—either in individual study or in a study group.

Classics have staying power. Although they were written in a particular place and time and often in response to situations different than our own, they deal with problems, concerns, and themes that transcend time and place.

The faithful of all generations have found spiritual nourishment in the Scriptures and in the works of Christians from earlier generations. Martin Luther and John Calvin would not have become who they were apart from their reading Augustine. God used the writings of Martin Luther to move John Wesley from a religion of dead works to an experience at Aldersgate in which his "heart was strangely warmed."

It is an awesome sight—these streams of gracious influence flowing from generation to generation.

Shepherd's Notes—Classics Series will help you take the first steps in claiming and drawing strength from your spiritual heritage.

Shepherd's Notes is designed to bridge the gap between now and then and to help you understand, love, and benefit from the company of saints of an earlier time. Each volume gives you an overview of the main themes dealt with by the author and then walks with you step-by-step through the classic.

Enjoy!
In Him,

David R. Shepherd
Editor-in-Chief

HOW TO USE THIS BOOK

DESIGNED FOR THE BUSY USER

Shepherd's Notes for Lewis's *Mere Christianity* is designed to provide an easy-to-use tool for gaining a quick overview of the major themes and the structure of *Mere Christianity*.

Shepherd's Notes are designed for laymen, pastors, teachers, small-group leaders and participants, as well as the classroom student.

DESIGNED FOR QUICK ACCESS

Persons with time restraints will especially appreciate the timesaving features built into *Shepherd's Notes*. All features are designed to work together to aid a quick and profitable encounter with *Mere Christianity*—to point the reader to sections in *Mere Christianity* where they may want to spend more time and go deeper.

Book-at-a-Glance. Provides a listing of the major sections of the *Mere Christianity*.

Summary. Each book of *Mere Christianity* is summarized section by section.

Shepherd's Notes—Commentary. Following the summary of the book, a commentary is provided. This enables the reader to look back and see the major themes that make up that particular book.

Icons. Various icons in the margin provide information to help the reader better understand that part of the text. Icons include:

Shepherd's Notes Icon. This icon denotes the commentary section of each book of *Mere Christianity*.

Scripture Icon. Scripture verses often illuminate passages in *Mere Christianity*.

Historical Background Icon. Many passages in *Mere Christianity* are better understood in the light of historical, cultural, biographical, and geographical information.

 Quotes Icon. This icon marks significant quotes from *Mere Christianity*.

 Points to Ponder Icon. These questions and suggestions for further thought will be especially useful in helping both individuals and groups see the relevance of *Mere Christianity* for our time.

INTRODUCTION

Clive Staples Lewis, known the world over as C. S. Lewis, is the most famous defender of the Christian faith in the twentieth century. He was born in Belfast, Ireland, in 1898, the second son of Albert James Lewis and Flora Augusta Hamilton Lewis. Lewis talked about the emotional aspects of his family in *Surprised by Joy*, his spiritual autobiography up to 1931. His parents married in 1894. His brother Warren was born in 1895.

His father graduated from Lurgan College and became a solicitor—an attorney who advises clients and represents them in the lower courts. Albert Lewis was emotional and frequently unhappy. He was absorbed with politics. Clive disliked both the intense interest in politics and his emotional fluctuation. Lewis was indifferent to politics all his life, and his father's emotionalism left him apprehensive of outward exhibitions of feelings.

Lewis' mother graduated from Queen's College, Belfast, with a first-class degree in logic and a second-class in mathematics. She was happy and affectionate. She died in early August 1908 when Lewis was not yet ten years old.

Lewis spent two years, ages sixteen to eighteen, with W. T. Kirkpatrick as tutor, a well-known, if ruthless, teacher. Kirkpatrick wrote to Albert Lewis that Clive Staples could aspire to a career as a writer or a scholar but that he had little chance of succeeding at anything else. Whether the statement was true, it turned out to be almost prophetic. In the winter of 1916, Lewis went to Oxford to sit for entrance examinations

"If all the world were Christian, it might not matter if all the world were educated. But, as it is, a cultural life will exist outside the Church whether it exists inside or not. To be ignorant and simple now—not to be able to meet the enemies on their own ground—would be to throw down our weapons, and to betray our uneducated brethren who have, under God, no defense but us against the intellectual attacks of the heathen. Good philosophy must exist, if for no other reason, because bad philosophy needs to be answered"—C. S. Lewis, *The Weight of Glory and Other Addresses.*

The "rumor" is that Magdalen College, Cambridge, offered Lewis this professorship because he had been "snubbed" by Magdalen College, Oxford, and passed over time and again for a professorship because of colleagues' jealousy of the great success of his Christian writings. Thus, the college with the same name in Cambridge offered Lewis the professorship, in part, to put Oxford in its place.

and thus began a lifelong association with Oxford and Cambridge.

The first part of his Oxford degree was in Greek and Latin; the second, in philosophy. Because competition for teaching, or tutorial, positions was so fierce, Lewis was advised to take on a third area of study, so he read English language and literature. In one year he completed a three-year course, including learning Anglo-Saxon (Old English). Thus, he held three first-class degrees from Oxford. When he finally found a temporary appointment in philosophy, his first lecture was attended by only four students. In 1925, Lewis was awarded an English fellowship at Magdalen College, Oxford, where he stayed until January 1, 1955, when he went to Magdalen College, Cambridge, as professor of medieval and Renaissance literature. He held this position for seven and one-half years until July 1963, when he resigned because of poor health.

During World War II, Lewis became a champion of orthodox Christianity. He saw his "mission" as a defender in a spiritual warfare that was raging in contemporary culture. His "war service" was to fight for what he believed to be true. This is why he traveled to Royal Air Force bases in 1940 and 1941 giving lectures on Christianity to servicemen.

Television as we know it was not yet. The first public television broadcasts were made in England in 1927 and in the United States in 1930. Regular broadcasting service began in the U.S. on April 30, 1939, in connection with the opening of the New York World's Fair. Scheduled broadcasting was interrupted by World

War II, and not until after the war was service resumed by a few broadcasting stations.

World War II brought many things to the United Kingdom, and one was a new openness to religion. The complacency toward organized religion, often found in a time of peace, was shattered, as were the foundations of many lives. Most people were still reading books, and all of a sudden Christian publishers found people ready to read books on religion.

C. S. Lewis did become a scholar and writer. Together his books have sold millions of copies. For example, *The Problem of Pain,* published in 1940, had already undergone twenty hard-cover printings by 1974 and continues to be a best-seller. *The Screwtape Letters* was reprinted eight times before the end of 1942, and the paperback editions were at one million by 1987. C. S. Lewis Societies continue around the world, especially in the United States; they hold regular meetings to read and discuss his work. Books about Lewis are also popular, as is almost any information about the man.

What is important about C. S. Lewis is that he was committed to defending and helping us understand basic Christianity. A writer for *Harper's* magazine once said: "The point about reading C. S. Lewis is that he makes you sure, whatever you believe, that religion accepted or rejected means something extremely serious, demanding the entire energy of the mind." By the late 1980s, the annual sales of the fifty or so books Lewis wrote approached two million dollars a year, with about half accounted for by the Narnia chronicles. Millions of people have been affected by reading Lewis's books.

At the end of 1946, there were twelve television stations operating on a commercial basis in the United States; by 1948, there were forty-six stations, and construction had begun on seventy-eight more, with more than three hundred applications submitted to the Federal Communications Commission for permits to build new stations.

A Biographical Time Line of Clive Staples Lewis

1898	Clive Staples Lewis born in Belfast, Ireland, on November 29, the second son of Albert James Lewis, a solicitor, and Flora Augusta Hamilton Lewis. Brother, Warren, was three years older.
1905	The family moved to "Little Lea," a large new house. Lewis later wrote: "I am the product of long corridors, empty sunlit rooms, upstairs indoor silences, attics explored in solitude . . . also of endless books."
1908	Mother, Flora, died of cancer on August 23. Lewis prayed for God to keep his mother alive. When she died, he blamed God.
1908–1910	In September 1908, both Lewis brothers were sent to England to Wynyard (Belsen) to school, in Watford, Hertfordshire. This was a terrible experience, in part, because of a brutal headmaster who was later declared insane.
1910	That autumn Lewis attended Campbell College near his home in Ireland for half a term. He left because of illness and because his father did not like the school.
1911	From January 1911 to the summer of 1913, Lewis returned to England to attend a preparatory school named Cherbourg House (Chartres) in Malvern. During this period, Lewis decided he was no longer a Christian. He became quite "worldly," discovered Wagner's music, and began to write poems and political history.
1913	Lewis won a classical scholarship to Malvern College and attended from September 1913 to July 1914. He wrote an atheistic tragedy in Greek form. He came to hate the school and had his father take him out.
1914	In the spring Lewis met Joseph Arthur Greeves. They became lifelong friends and corresponded through letters for forty-nine years.
1914–1916	Lewis studied with W. T. Kirkpatrick, who helped prepare him for entrance to the University of Oxford. He studied Greek, Latin, French, German, and Italian. He also read in English and American literature, listened to music, and wrote poetry and romance in prose.
1915	In October, he read George MacDonald's *Phantastes*. MacDonald was to have a great impact on his later life.

A Biographical Time Line of Clive Staples Lewis

1916 In December he sat for a classical scholarship at Oxford and was admitted to University College. He loved it.

1917 From January to March Lewis continued to study under Kirkpartick. His lack of ability in mathematics caused him to fail. On April 28, he went to Oxford; but before the end of term, he was recruited into the army to serve in World War I. During this time he made friends with E. F. C. (Paddy) Moore and later with his mother, Janie King Moore. Later, when Paddy was killed, Lewis became a son to Mrs. Moore, who was a widow. This relationship continued until 1951 when she died. On September 25, 1917, he was commissioned a second lieutenant in the Somerset Light Infantry. He arrived on the front lines of France on his nineteenth birthday.

1918 He was hospitalized in January, suffering from trench fever. He rejoined his battalion on March 4 and brought in about sixty German soldiers as prisoners. He was wounded in action at Mount Bernenchon and again went to the hospital on April 14. On May 22, he returned to the hospital in England. On June 16, he was released from the hospital and went to visit the Kirkpatricks at Great Bookham.

1919 In January he returned to University College, Oxford, and began to make many lifelong friends, including Owen Barfield, a student at Wadham College, Oxford. He published *Spirits in Bondage*, his first book, a small collection of lyric poems, under the name of Clive Hamilton.

1920 In the spring he took a First-Class Honours degree in Mods. from Oxford University.

1921 Lewis made his first visit to W. B. Yeats' home on March 14.

1922 In April he began to write *Dymer*, a long narrative poem. He also began a verse version of *Till We Have Faces*. He took an Oxford First-Class Honours degree in Greats.

1923 He took an Oxford First in English and won the Chancellor's Prize.

1924 He began tutorial work at University College in philosophy for one year.

A Biographical Time Line of Clive Staples Lewis

1925	He was elected to a Fellowship in English Language and Literature at Magdalen College, Oxford, where he stayed until 1954. His friends included J. R. R. Tolkien, Nevill Coghill, H. V. D. Dyson, and A. C. Harwood, who later became members of the Inklings.
1926	Under the pen name Clive Hamilton, he published a book-length narrative poem *Dymer*. He claimed the story "arrived, complete" when he was in his seventeenth year.
1929	During Trinity Term, the third term of the academic year, Lewis confessed on his knees at Magdalen that "God is God." In September Lewis's father died in Belfast.
1930	In October Lewis and Mrs. Moore and her daughter settled at The Kilns, which was to be his home until his death.
1931	Lewis and his brother started out on motorcycle to visit a zoo thirty miles east of Oxford. He later said that when they started out he did not believe that Jesus Christ was the Son of God but when they reached the zoo he did. He was thirty-three years old.
1933	*The Pilgrim's Regress: An Allegorical Apology for Christianity, Reason and Romanticism* was published.
1936	*The Allegory of Love: A Study in Medieval Tradition,* for which he won the Hawthornden Prize, was published. Shortly after, Lewis and Charles Williams began correspondence, which led to a close friendship.
1937	Lewis won the Gollancz Memorial Prize.
1938	*Out of the Silent Planet* was published.
1939	*The Personal Heresy: A Controversy*, a debate with E. M. W. Tillyard, master of Jesus College, Cambridge, was published. Lewis believed poetry should be objective and impersonal. Oxford University Press moved to Oxford, and Charles Williams, who worked for the press, also came to Oxford. Lewis and Williams remained close friends until Williams' death on May 15, 1945. *Rehabilitations and Other Essays*, a collection of studies of English writers, of British education, etc., was published.
1940	*The Problem of Pain* was published.

A Biographical Time Line of Clive Staples Lewis

1940–
1941
Lewis was the wartime lecturer on Christianity for the Royal Air Force.

1941
Lewis helped form the Socratic Club at Oxford and became a longtime president. On August 6, Lewis began his first of twenty-five talks on the BBC radio.

1942
Broadcast Talks: Reprinted with Some Alterations from Two Series of Broadcast Talks ("Right and Wrong: A Clue to the Meaning of the Universe" and "What Christians Believe") Given in 1941 and 1942—later revised, these become the first two parts of *Mere Christianity*. *The Screwtape Letters* was published. Also *A Preface to 'Paradise Lost', Being the Ballard Matthews Lectures Delivered at University College, North Wales* was published.

1943
Christian Behaviour: A Further Series of Broadcast Talks was published. Later, in revised form, it became the third part of *Mere Christianity*. *Perelandra* was published. *The Abolition of Man, or Reflections on Education with Special Reference to the Teaching of English in the Upper Forms of Schools* was published, originally three lectures at Durham University.

1944
Beyond Personality: The Christian Idea of God was published. Later revised, it became the last part of *Mere Christianity*.

1945
That Hideous Strength: A Modern Fairy-Story for Grown-ups was published. This was the last volume in the "science fiction" trilogy.

1946
Lewis was awarded the doctorate of divinity by St. Andrews University. He published *George MacDonald: An Anthology*. MacDonald probably had a greater impact on Lewis than any other writer.

1947
Miracles: A Preliminary Study was published.

1948
Arthurian Torso: Containing the Posthumous Fragment of "The Figure of Arthur" by Charles Williams and a Commentary on the Arthurian Poems of Charles Williams by C. S. Lewis was published.

1949
Transposition and Other Addresses was published, containing some of Lewis's finest essays. The American title was *The Weight of Glory and Other Addresses*.

A Biographical Time Line of Clive Staples Lewis

1950	*The Lion, the Witch and the Wardrobe* was published—the first of the seven Chronicles of Narnia children's stories. Lewis was fifty-two years of age.
1951	*Prince Caspian: The Return to Narnia* was published, the second Chronicle. Lewis was offered the honor of Commander of the Order of the British Empire by the prime minister, but he kindly refused. Mrs. Moore died.
1952	Doctorate of literature awarded Lewis, *in absentia* by Laval University, Quebec, on September 22. *Mere Christianity* and *The Voyage of the 'Dawn Treader'* were published, the third Chronicle. Reepicheep, the gallant mouse is seeking Aslan's country.
1953	*The Silver Chair* was published, the fourth Chronicle.
1954	*The Horse and His Boy* was published, the fifth Chronicle. *English Literature in the Sixteenth Century, Excluding Drama*, originally in the Clark Lecture series at Trinity College, Cambridge, was published.
1954	Lewis left Oxford after almost thirty years to accept the professorship of medieval and Renaissance literature at Magdalene College, Cambridge.
1955	*Surprised by Joy: The Shape of My Early Life*, his autobiography detailing his life up to 1931, was published. *The Magician's Nephew* was published, the sixth Chronicle.
1956	*The Last Battle* was published, the seventh Chronicle of Narnia. In a legal ceremony Lewis and Joy Davidman Gresham were married on April 23. Lewis and Joy later had an "ecclesiastical marriage" in January 1957. Joy had cancer of the thigh.
1958	*Reflections on the Psalms* was published.
1960	*The Four Loves* was published. *Studies in Words*, lectures given at Cambridge, were published. An American publisher brought together seven essays as *The World's Last Night and Other Essays*. On July 13, two months after they returned from a visit to Greece, Joy died.
1961	*A Grief Observed* was published under the pen name of N. W. Clerk. Also published was *An Experiment in Criticism*.
1962	*They Asked for a Paper: Papers and Addresses* was published.

A Biographical Time Line of Clive Staples Lewis

1963   In July Lewis went into a coma but recovered. He resigned his
        professorship at Cambridge. On November 22, C. S. Lewis died at
        The Kilns only seven days short of his sixty-fifth birthday.

1964   *Letters to Malcolm: Chiefly on Prayer* was published posthumously.
        It was the last book Lewis prepared for the press.

INTRODUCTION TO
MERE CHRISTIANITY

This new openness to religion as a result of
WWII caused the British Broadcasting Corpo-
ration (the famous BBC) to ask Lewis to broadcast radio talks for them. On August 6, 1941,
Lewis began his first series of live radio talks in
two parts. These were an immediate success,
and many listeners wrote letters to Lewis; and,
as if a moral duty, he wrote replies to most of
them. The second series of radio messages was
in 1942, and the third in 1944. Thus the material which makes up *Mere Christianity* was first
presented to the public as a series of radio
messages.

Later these were published in three parts—the
first part as *The Case for Christianity* (first published in England under the title *Broadcast Talks*)
and the second as *Christian Behaviour*, both in
1943. The third was originally published as
Beyond Personality in 1945. Lewis made a few
additions to the radio version in the printed text,
but the printed version is substantially the same.
When Lewis prepared the radio version for
print, he decided to keep the conversational
form, contractions and colloquialisms, his ver-
bal emphasis by italics, etc. Later he came to
think this a mistake, calling it "an undesirable
hybrid between the art of speaking and the art of
writing" (preface). In the paperback edition he

"Members of several
churches proclaim
that 'of course C. S.
Lewis was one of us.'
In fact C.S. Lewis was
a Christian not given
to 'isms,' and whilst he
preferred to attend the
local Anglican church,
this was more a
matter of convenience
than of conviction. It
was from him that I
learnt that
*Sectarianism is one of
the Devil's keenest
weapons against
Christendom*"
[emphasis
added]—Doughlas H.
Gresham, *Lenten
Lands*.

changed the italics for spoken emphasis, and material he thought he understood better ten years later was altered as was some material that had been misunderstood in the original.

Richard Baxter (1615–91) was the most prolific writer of the Puritan divines. Born in Rowton, Shropshire, England, he attended the free school at Wroxeter but attained his education largely through self-instruction, private tutelage, and introspection. He was known for his work as a minister and his approximately two hundred writings. Among these are *The Saints' Everlasting Rest* (1650), *The Reformed Pastor* (1656), *A Call to the Unconverted* (1657), *Methodus Theologiae Christianae* (1681), and *Reliquiae Baxterianae* (1695) his autobiography. His writings are filled with zeal for the lost, genuine piety, and a desire for reconciliation of the warring division of Christians in his day. Baxter believed that mere Christianity meant the basic form and beliefs of Christianity accepted by orthodox believers of all traditions and denominations.

The combination of the three books as *Mere Christianity* happened in 1952. Lewis explained his reason for writing in the preface. He made clear, by way of a warning, that the book offers no help for those who are trying to decide between different Christian denominations. This is because his intent was to do a service for his "unbelieving neighbours" by explaining and defending what he thought had been shared by most all Christians since the beginning. This approach was justified in three ways: (1) He was not an expert on the points of division, which are usually the result of theology or church history. (2) Experts have already spent much time arguing over such matters. (3) These disputed points do not bring unbelievers to Christ. In fact, the more we argue over them, the more likely unbelievers are going to stay just that. Lewis's agenda was clearly to defend what the seventeenth-century Christian writer, Richard Baxter, called "mere" Christianity. This is where Lewis got the phrase.

Readers are cautioned not to "draw fanciful inferences" from his "silence on certain disputed matters." One cannot even tell from his silence whether Lewis thought the issue was important. Christians disagree also about the importance of their disagreements. Before long, what has started out as a "mere disagreement" has become "absolutely essential." In an attempt to keep to "mere Christianity," Lewis sent the original script of Book II to an Anglican, a Methodist, a Presbyterian, and a Roman Catholic for criticism. He noted that the Methodist thought he had not treated faith enough and the Catholic thought Lewis had gone too far in claiming the different theories of the atonement as comparatively unimportant. With these exceptions noted, all five were agreed.

Book III considers questions related to morals. Here Lewis was also silent on some issues but for another reason. He was reluctant to talk much about temptations to which he was not exposed. He gave as examples gambling, for which he never had any interest, and birth-control—as he was not a woman, married (at this point), or even a priest. From his experience in World War I, he never liked people who give "exhortations to men on the front line" while they were "in ease and safety."

He heard more serious objections regarding his use of the word *Christian* and how it is defined. Who was Lewis to say that one has to believe certain doctrines to be called a Christian? The old ruse of the "character issue" was raised: Might not a person who doesn't believe Lewis's set of doctrines be much more in the "spirit of Christ" and therefore more truly Christian? But Lewis pointed out strongly that one cannot "without disaster, use language as these objectors want . . . to use it." He referenced the word *gentleman,* which in the past had a specific meaning and is now little more than a compliment. "When a word ceases to be a term of description and becomes merely a term of praise, it no longer tells you facts about the object: It only tells you about the speaker's attitude to that object."

IMPACT OF THE WORK

The work was copyrighted by The Macmillan Company in 1943, 1945, and 1952 and was

C. S. Lewis "remained aware that progress in the practice of Christianity is both necessary and difficult. 'I am appalled . . . to see how much of the change I thought I had undergone lately was only imaginary. The real work seems still to be done.' He discovered that even the act of writing required the valley of humiliation. . . . Lewis warned that the yen to publish is spiritually dangerous. 'One must reach the point of "not caring two straws about his own status" before he can wish wholly for God's kingdom, not his own, to be established.' Death to ambition as such will be the beginning of new life. Above all, the part of a man which puts success first must be humiliated if a man is ever to be really free.

produced in a paperback edition in 1960. By 1969, this edition already had ten printings. Lewis's writings have sold millions and unquestionably affected tens of thousands of people. One example directly related to this present work is the impact it had on Charles Colson who was imprisoned for his part in the Watergate scandal of Richard Nixon. While in prison, Colson read *Mere Christianity* and was struck by the logic of its defense of Christianity and its exposure of human pride. He said that reading *Mere Christianity* was an important step in his conversion.

Book I has five chapters, each treating some question regarding the "Law of Human Nature." These were the first part of the two parts given as a radio address in the autumn of 1941. Here Lewis attempted to establish that we have an innate sense of law, of right and wrong, and that we need to have a belief in God for that sense to take on any real meaning. Chapter 1 is a direct discussion of the law. Chapter 2 treats some objections. Chapter 3 looks at what Lewis called the reality of the law. Chapter 4 discusses what lies behind the law of nature and the possible explanations for the existence of the universe. Chapter 5 discusses the implications of the existence of natural law with regard to both human and divine "goodness" and explains why an understanding of natural law is necessary before one can see the need for Christianity.

CHAPTER 1: THE LAW OF HUMAN NATURE

Chapter at a Glance

Chapter 1 contains an argument for a universal standard of behavior. Lewis made two points: (1) Humans everywhere have a "curious idea" that they should behave in a certain way. We cannot rid ourselves of it. (2) Yet, as humans, we do not, in fact, behave in the way we know we should. We know the law of nature but break it.

Summary

The chapter starts with Lewis's reminding us that everyday quarrels happen with children

13

Natural law—In ethics, the idea that there are natural moral laws known by all, moral order divinely implanted and accessible to all human beings by way of reason. All beings come under the regulation of this eternal law. Thus all things are inclined toward their proper acts and ends by divine reason. Men and animals share in this divine regulation. To avoid confusion with the law of nature, we call the part of the eternal law which applied especially to the free acts of man, the "natural moral law." *Natural law* is not made by human reason but is naturally implanted in the reason of man by God—Miethe, *The Compact Dictionary of Doctrinal Terms*.

and adults, both educated and uneducated. Some of the examples remind us of what we think are rights and/or valid expectations. Examples: treating people in a way you would like to be treated, getting there "first" means you get the seat, receiving a piece of fruit in exchange for the one we gave, and keeping promises. This chapter reminds us that we believe in the validity of such actions and reactions because we think other people also know and share a common standard of behavior. He pointed out that the quarrel is not usually over the standard but the action, which is justified by the offender as some exception to the standard.

Both participants in the dispute seem to have in mind a law or rule of fair play or decent behavior as a basis for their argument or discussion. Otherwise they wouldn't quarrel but would fight like animals. The act of quarrelling is an attempt to show that one of the participants is wrong. This would make no sense, said Lewis, unless there was some agreement about what is really right and wrong. He reminded us that even games—like football—make sense only if there are rules by which to play.

The idea of a law or rule about right and wrong used to be called the law of nature. Now the term *laws of nature* usually refers to physical laws of nature, heredity, or chemistry, not the law of *human* nature. The difference between the *law of nature* and the *laws of nature* is that a man can choose to disobey the law of nature whereas the laws of nature—such as gravity—must be obeyed. Lewis also believed that when you find people who claim to believe there is no real right and wrong, you don't have to observe them long before you see that they *do*, in fact, believe that some things are "wrong." Example: A person might not think he has to keep a promise to you, but wait until you break one to him! History may be full of nations that broke treaties with us, but just wait until we want to break one with them. Even if the other nation argued that the particular treaty they want to break is unfair, how, if treaties do not matter—there is no such thing as right and wrong, no law of nature—can there be such an idea as fair or unfair.

COMMENTARY

Lewis said that the real impressive thing, when we look carefully, is the similarity between moral views, not the differences.

Thus, Lewis was not the first person to argue that there was an innate moral law inside human beings or that this fact leads to a supreme being. Although Immanuel Kant (1724–1804) rejected the idea that one could use theoretical proofs to establish God's existence, he did argue that humans must "act" as if God exists to make sense of our moral experience.

CHAPTER 2: SOME OBJECTIONS

Chapter at a Glance

After the original live radio broadcast of "The Law of Human Nature," Lewis received several letters objecting that what he was calling moral law was really only instinct or social convention. Chapter 2 argues that the "Rule of Decent Behaviour" is far more than human instinct.

Summary

Chapter 2 starts by reminding us that two facts are foundational: People all over the world have this curious idea of moral law; and yet people don't behave accordingly. Before he went on to other subjects, Lewis addressed some of the objections he had received in letters.

The first general objection was that moral law was simply human herd instinct. Lewis didn't deny that humans have herd instinct, but he vigorously denied that this is what he was calling moral law. He made three points:

1. Feeling a desire to act in a certain way—say, the desire to help—is different from the feeling that we ought to help even if we really don't want to do so. In the case of a cry for help, we will normally feel two desires—the herd instinct to help and the instinct of self-preservation, to keep out of danger. We also find inside a feeling that tells us we ought to follow the help instinct. Clearly, the thing which judges between the two instincts is neither of them.

2. Moral law is not simply one of our instincts. When two instincts come into conflict, the stronger does not always win! In fact, said Lewis, moral law usually seems to tell us to side with the weaker impulse and to try to make it the stronger. He gave the example of a drowning man. Surely we prefer to be safe, but we help anyway. Clearly we are not acting from instinct.

3. If the moral law were only one of our many instincts, we should be able to point to an impulse which is always good, but we cannot. Even a mother's love or patriotism are not always good, as sex or fighting are not always bad. Lewis said that really there are no such things as good or bad impulses. This point, wrote Lewis, has great practical consequence. He said that the most dangerous thing we could do is to take any one impulse and make it the absolute we should follow no matter what. Any

one impulse made into an absolute guide will actually make us into devils.

Second general objection: Other people wrote saying that what Lewis was calling moral law is just social convention, something learned through education. But just because something can be taught and/or learned doesn't make it a mere human invention. Multiplication tables, for example, can be learned; but they are real truths not just something people devised. Lewis said that we can and do learn the Rule of Decent Behaviour; some things we can learn are real truths.

COMMENTARY

Often when secular psychologists, sociologists, and anthropologists in the recent past have tried to argue that there is no such thing as an objective moral law and all this stuff we think is moral law is nothing more than herd instinct or social convention, they are looking only on the surface at human behavior. Yes, social convention has been different and does change widely over time, even generation to generation; but, when we look more closely, we will see just how similar basic moral views have been throughout time.

If "social convention" is something learned but does change from time to time and generation to generation, how can we decide whether something *is* a social convention or God's law, something that is an ethical absolute established by God?

CHAPTER 3: THE REALITY OF THE LAW

Chapter at a Glance

Chapter 3 argues that the laws of nature are not really laws at all but only an explanation of how physical things work. On the other hand, the law of human nature, or moral law, tells us what people ought to do but don't do. We begin to realize there is more than one kind of reality.

In philosophy *ought* implies *can*. When one is told that he ought to do something, it would make no ethical sense unless that action can actually be carried out. Thus, ethics is concerned with what we *ought* to do which, in a sense, is the theory behind action; but it is also concerned that the theory can be consistently applied in everyday action.

The statement: "Remember: a clear conscience is nothing more than a bad memory" points, in part, to the reality of moral law. C. S. Lewis understood that God's mark was on us, and yet no one has a clear conscience. What is the role of the church in helping individual Christians with their conscience?

Summary

An important distinction is made between the laws of nature and natural law. It turns out that the laws of nature aren't laws at all. These so-called "laws" are only descriptions of the way natural things—like a stone, a tree, or the weather—have to work. These laws of nature only mean what nature actually does. But the law of human nature, or the law of decent behavior, is something different. It doesn't tell us *what* we do but how we *ought* to act.

This rule of right and wrong is something really there and not something we made up. Lewis went next to his most important conclusion: The moral law is real but it is not a physical reality.

 COMMENTARY

Christians do not believe that we should do, or not do, a particular thing just because it is useful for us as individuals or for the human race to do so—for example, to be nice. This may be a factor in choosing an action, but the real question for the Christians with regard to a particular action is: Is it right according to the teachings of Jesus and the Scripture? The reality of moral law for the Christian is a matter of what God Himself has implanted in us and our further understanding of the ethical teaching of the Bible.

Already by the end of this chapter, we have arrived at more than one kind of reality. In actuality, only Christians understand the nature of both kinds of reality. All of those "tugs on the heart," with which we were drawn to act against our selfish nature before becoming Christians, only begin to make sense after we have traveled down the road with Christ. Only then can we begin to understand both the reality of moral law and its Source!

CHAPTER 4: WHAT LIES BEHIND THE LAW

Chapter at a Glance

Lewis concluded that there must be more than one kind of reality—something above and beyond the ordinary facts of behavior but still real. Next he considered what this means, what it tells us about our world, our universe. Two views are discussed: the materialist view and the religious view.

Summary

This chapter starts by summing up what has been arrived at in chapter 3. Now we must see what this tells us about our world. Lewis noted that men have two views about what the universe is and how it came to exist: the materialist view and the religious view. People who hold the materialist view believe matter and space just happened or have always existed, and no one really knows why. Human beings, thinking creatures, were produced by some fluke.

According to the religious view, something is behind the universe which is more like mind than anything else. In other words, it is at least intelligent. At the very least, it is conscious, has purposes, and chooses between options. This mind made the universe at least in part so that it could create creatures like itself—creatures with minds.

Both views have been there from the beginning. Science in the ordinary sense cannot tell us which is the correct view. This is not due to the

The nature and definition of *science* are important: "The modern mind" or "the new science" defines what constitutes "science" in terms of a restrictive methodology. *Science* is synonymous with the method of observing repeatable phenomena in a laboratory. Thus science must involve proof and certainty, must not depart from what can be generated rigorously from immediate observation, and must not speculate beyond presently observable processes. Given this definition of, or limitation on, *science,* it is clear why such a method cannot answer "ultimate" questions or questions regarding prehistory.

inadequacy of the evidence but because of the limitations of science, or perhaps of the scientific method itself. Science works by experiments which can and must be able to be repeated in the laboratory. Thus science as science cannot say whether there is or is not something behind nature. Why there is a universe or whether it has meaning are not questions for which science can give an answer.

 COMMENTARY

If C. S. Lewis was correct, moral law itself is evidence of more than one kind of Reality. Atheists often ask, "What is the evidence of the so-called 'spiritual' in physical reality?" And before even an attempt at an answer can be given, they loudly affirm, "There is none!" According to the atheist, everything in existence is reducible to physical matter; the only reality is natural, material, and mechanical. Moral law is not the only evidence for this "other kind of reality"; there are many arguments for the existence of God and for the Christian worldview.

CHAPTER 5: WE HAVE CAUSE TO BE UNEASY

Chapter at a Glance

Critics claim religion has already been tried, and it failed. So don't try to turn back the clock. Lewis made three comments: (1) You can put the clock back, and should, if the clock is wrong! (2) So far the argument has only shown that there is Something behind moral law. (3) He was not trying to trick his hearers/readers. His point was that Christianity really does not

"The wrath of God is being revealed from heaven against all the godlessness and wickedness of men who suppress the truth by their wickedness, since what may be known about God is plain to them, because God has made it plain to them. For since the creation of the world God's invisible qualities—his eternal power and divine nature—have been clearly seen, being understood from what has been made, so that men are without excuse. For although they knew God, they neither glorified him as God nor gave thanks to him, but their thinking became futile and their foolish hearts were darkened. Although they claimed to be wise, they became fools and exchanged the glory of the immortal God for images made to look like mortal man and birds and animals and reptiles" (Rom. 1:18–23).

make sense until you face the facts he has out-lined so far.

Summary

Chapter 5 starts with how his readers may, at this point in the discussion, have reacted to the progression of his argument. Some may have become annoyed because they think his philo-sophical discussion has turned into a "religious jaw." *Progress* is defined as "getting nearer to the place where you want to be." Therefore, if we have made a mistake, simply going forward will not get us there. We may have to correct our course.

Perhaps the most important thing we can learn about the Being behind the universe by observ-ing the moral law within us is that He "is intensely interested in right conduct—in fair play, unselfishness, courage, good faith, honesty and truthfulness." Therefore we can now agree with Christianity, and certain other religions, that this God is good. Lewis observed: "But do not let us go too fast here. The Moral Law does not give us any grounds for thinking that God is 'good' in the sense of being indulgent, or soft, or sympathetic. There is nothing indulgent about the Moral Law. It is as hard as nails. . . . If God is like the Moral Law, then He is not soft" (p. 37). One gets no idea of a forgiving God here! Lewis believed only a person can forgive, and we haven't gotten to a personal God yet. This God may be strictly impersonal mind.

"Some people talk as if meeting the gaze of absolute goodness would be fun. They need to think again. They are still only playing with religion. Goodness is either the great safety or the great danger— according to the way you react to it. And we have reacted the wrong way" (p. 38).

In fact, if there is such "an absolute goodness," it must abhor most of the actions of humans. This puts us in a "terrible fix" because it puts us in a universe were God is the only comfort but at the same time the supreme terror. He is what we

"The Christian church is not a society of integrated personalities, nor of philosophers, nor of mystics, nor even of good people. It is a society of broken personalities, of men and women with troubled minds, of people who know that they are not good. The Christian church is a society of sinners. It is the only society in the world, membership in which is based upon the single qualification that the candidate shall be unworthy of membership"
—Charles Clayton Morrison, *What Is Christianity,* 211.

"Therefore, as God's chosen people, holy and dearly loved, clothe yourselves with compassion, kindness, humility, gentleness and patience. Bear with each other and forgive whatever grievances you may have against one another. Forgive as the Lord forgave you. And over all these virtues put on love, which binds them all together in perfect unity" (Col. 3:12–14).

need most, but we have made ourselves His enemies.

 COMMENTARY

For Christianity to make sense, we must *face* many facts, not the least of which is our own selfishness. This Lewis will treat in more depth in Book IV. But here he made the important point that Christianity is about repentance and forgiveness. First, we must as individuals come to grips with our own need to be forgiven! Until we do this, we are not likely to understand Christianity.

BOOK II: WHAT CHRISTIANS BELIEVE

Book at a Glance
Book II has five chapters. The first discusses
rival concepts of God: atheism, pantheism, the
Christian view. Chapter 2 discusses dualism and
"The Invasion" by the Rightful King. Chapter 3
is about the problem of evil, free will, and the
shocking alternative: God sends the Redeemer.
Chapter 4 treats the doctrines of repentance and
the atonement and that only Christ can be "The
Perfect Penitent." Chapter 5 is a discussion of
the practical conclusion: how the new life is
spread, the responsibility of a Christian here,
and why God has delayed landing in force.

CHAPTER 1: THE RIVAL CONCEPTIONS OF GOD

Chapter at a Glance
Lewis offered one thing Christians don't have to
believe. A discussion of the differences between
the majority of people in history who have
believed in a God or gods and modern atheism
follows. The difference between pantheism and
the Christian idea of God is discussed. If such a
good God exists, why is there so much suffering
and evil in the world?

Summary
Lewis had been asked to tell his audience what
Christians believe. Yet he started by relating
the one thing Christians do not have to believe:
that other religions are completely wrong. An
atheist has to believe that the main point of all
religions is "one huge mistake." Christians are
free to think that all religions contain at least
some hint of truth. At least in this, Christians

Pantheism—From the Greek *pan*, "all" and *theos*, "god." The worldview that denies God's transcendence and teaches that the substance of God and the substance of the physical universe are in some sense identical; reality is composed of a single being of which all things are modes, moments, members, appearances, or projections. Classical Hinduism is pantheistic as were the philosophies of Benedict Spinoza (1632–1677) and G. W. F. Hegel (1770–1831).

are able to take a more open view than atheists. When it comes to differences between Christianity and other religions, Christianity is thought correct, of course, and the other religions wrong. The example of mathematics is again used. Even though there is only one correct answer, some wrong answers are closer to being correct than others.

When discussing humanity as a whole, there are two "big divisions": (1) into majority and minority. The majority—the ancient Greeks and Romans, Platonists, Stoics, Hindus, Muslims, animists, and Christians—believe in some kind of God or gods. Modern Western European materialists are atheists and are in the minority. (2) The next is with regard to the kind of God believed in. Here there are two seriously different concepts:

1. God is beyond good and evil. The first view is called *pantheism*.

2. The other view is held by Jews, Muslims, and Christians. In this view God is completely good or righteous, a God who really cares for people and takes sides, who wants humans to behave in a certain way. The Christian view of God is very different from pantheism.

In the Christian view, God created the universe. The analogy is given of the painter and the painting. The painter is not the picture. God *is* Creator of the world. He made all things, but He is separate from the created world. God made everything, but Christianity also teaches that many things have gone wrong with that world. Christianity teaches that God "insists very loudly" on putting everything back the way it was, putting it right again.

Atheism is "too simple." How could we have found out that the whole universe has no meaning if it truly had no meaning?

COMMENTARY

Lewis said that Christians do not have to believe that other religions are completely wrong, that some "hint" of truth exists in them. Modern atheism is a relatively "new" idea when seen in historical perspective.

CHAPTER 2: THE INVASION

Chapter at a Glance

Atheism is too simple! In chapter 2, Lewis considered another view which is also too simple—watered-down Christianity.

Summary

If atheism is too simple, so is the view called "Christianity-and-water." This view states that everything is all right because God is God, but it omits "the difficult and terrible" doctrines of sin, hell, the devil, and redemption. Simple religion is no good because "real things are not simple" even though they may appear to be. Examples, like the scientific explanation of a table and a child's prayer, are given to show that often what appears to be simple is in reality not so. Often atheists bring forth a young child's version of Christianity to attack. They consciously or unconsciously want to destroy Christianity. We are told to be on guard against such people because they change the ground of their argument from minute to minute and end up only wasting our time.

An honest atheist knows reality is complicated and will not try to take "cheap shots" at Christian

Atheism—From the Greek *atheos*, "godless," a word found only once in the New Testament, in Ephesians 2:12, the belief that there is no God. In the twentieth century, atheism has grown with the advance of Communism, an atheistic religion, and the establishment of atheist organizations such as the American Association for the Advancement of Atheism (1925), the League of Militant Atheists (1929), and with documents like *Humanist Manifesto I* (1933), *Humanist Manifesto II* (1973), and *A Secular Humanist Declaration* (1980)—Miethe, *The Compact Dictionary*, 37–38.

belief. Reality is not only complicated, but it is also not neat or obvious or what we anticipate. This is one reason Lewis *believed* Christianity! Lewis thought Christianity was not something we could have guessed beforehand. If it offered us just that kind of universe, we would feel it was being made up. Christianity is not what anyone would have made up. Rather, it has just the "queer twist" one would expect real things to have. Thus Lewis asked readers/listeners to leave behind "boy's philosophies" full of "over-simple answers."

Now to the problem—a universe which contains such bad and meaningless things but also has people who know that bad *is* bad and meaningless *is* meaningless. Only two views face all the facts. (1) The Christian view tells us that we live in a good world in which things have gone wrong, are not now as they should be. (2) Dualism believes that there are two equal and independent forces, one good and one evil, behind everything. Thus, we live on a battlefield in an endless war. Lewis believed that, apart from Christianity, dualism was the "manliest and most sensible" system "on offer," as the British say.

Dualism—From the Latin *duo*, "two." The idea that a reality has two fundamental parts or principles, often seen as opposing factors, such as matter and spirit or good and evil. Theological dualism is the belief that two gods are fighting for control of the universe—Miethe, *The Compact Dictionary*, 76.

But Lewis believed dualism has a "catch" in it. We must say that one of the two powers is actually good and one actually bad, not that we merely prefer one over the other. But once we have said this, we have added a third thing to the formula—some law, standard, rule of good to which one of the two conforms. And again we have a standard that is "farther back" or "higher" than the two. Thus, this Standard is the real God. And *good* and *bad* turn out to be in relation to this Ultimate Standard, this Real God.

Even if you look at it from the view of the bad power, the same point is true. The bad power, who is supposed to be equal with the good, also doesn't compare. He, too, is not independent. In fact, it turns out that he is part of the Good Power's world. Now we begin to understand why Christianity teaches that the devil is a fallen angel. This is not just a story for children; a realization that evil is a "parasite, not an original thing" is at the heart of this truth. A bad man, to be "effectively bad," uses things which are good in themselves—resolution, cleverness, good looks, existence itself; only he uses them for bad intents, bad ends. This is why, declared Lewis, dualism does not work.

Yet Lewis freely admitted that real Christianity comes much closer to dualism than some think. When he first read the New Testament, he was surprised how much talk there was about a "Dark Power" or "mighty evil spirit." This power is behind death, disease, and sin! But there is an important difference: Christianity believes this dark power was created good by God and somehow—according to Augustine by the sin of Pride—went wrong. Christianity and dualism agree that the universe is at war. But, for Christianity, it is not a war between independent powers but a rebellion. The world is "enemy-occupied territory."

"Christianity is the story of how the rightful king has landed . . . and is calling us all to take part in a great campaign of sabotage. When you go to church you are really listening-in to the secret wireless from our friends: that is why the enemy is so anxious to prevent us from going" (p. 51).

 COMMENTARY

Often people, even some Christians as well as some atheists, make the serious mistake of confusing the "simple" with the "simplistic." A belief system may have rather clear and *simple* principles or ideas, but this is far from saying that these are *simplistic*—either easy to comprehend or apply! Really "atheism" and the "Christianity-and-water" views are both "simple religion," for it turns out that atheists are just as religious as theists. They just have a different set of beliefs and/or presuppositions. The real question is which set of beliefs makes more sense out of, gives a more comprehensive fit to, the total experience of human beings! Lewis argued that the Christian worldview best informs and explains our experience.

CHAPTER 3: THE SHOCKING ALTERNATIVE

Chapter at a Glance

Here Lewis affirmed that an evil power has become the "Prince of this World." Problems are raised: Is this situation God's will or not? Either way you answer seems to have difficulties: If this is God's will, there is something quite strange in this. If it isn't the will of God, how do you account for all this given the fact that God is an absolute power? The implications of free will and where the dark power went wrong are discussed. Then the "real shock" is revealed: God sends the Redeemer.

Summary

Anyone who has been in authority knows how something can be both in accordance with your will and at the same time not. The example is given of a mother who wishes her children to be "tidy" but realizes that she cannot teach her children how to be tidy by doing it for them. She has to let them be free both to experience it—or the lack of it—and to learn for themselves. You may will something strongly, but the minute you make compliance voluntary, you have both willed it to be so and allowed it not to be so.

Just so, God created us with free will. We can do either right or wrong. Lewis could not imagine a really free creature who had no possibility of doing wrong. There is no sense in which a creature can be said to be truly free and not have the real option to choose bad as well as good. Why did God give us free will? Even though evil is made possible in free will, it is also the only way love, goodness, or real joy are possible.

God created humans with freedom of choice. This is consistent with the Christian Scriptures. John 3:16 reads: "For God so loved the world that He gave His one and only Son, that whoever believes in him shall not perish but have eternal life."

God knew not only the implications but also the results of this risky business of free will, that man would use it in the wrong way. Clearly, He believed the risk was worth taking! When we say that we can envision a better world than God created, we are really saying the Source of our reasoning power made a mistake in His reasoning! How ridiculous! When we really understand the implications of being created in God's image, of having free will, we will see how silly it is to argue that it could have been done better.

Lewis admitted that we cannot be absolutely sure about how this dark power went wrong. Yet the instant we have a "self," the possibility of putting that self at the center, of its wanting to be God, becomes a real possibility. Satan's sin and the sin he taught the human race was the sin of pride, that we could "be like gods," that we could somehow be independent of the real God, that we could be happy apart from Him.

God gave us (1) a conscience, a sense of right and wrong, a moral law deep within us. He also gave us, according to Lewis, (2) "good dreams," the idea of resurrection and new life. And, (3) He chose a particular people and spent centuries revealing the "sort of God He was" to them.

Now comes the real shock. God sends, in essence, Himself! A man is born who talks as if

He is God, says He can forgive sins, says He has always existed, even claims that He will judge the world in the end! This Jewish fellow could not be misunderstood by His fellow Jews. What He was claiming was clear to them. What this man claimed was the "most shocking thing . . . ever . . . uttered" by the lips of man.

Since we, today, have heard it so often, the claim to be able to forgive sins is inclined to slip past us unnoticed. But it really should not, for it is nothing short of "preposterous as to be comic" if not true. Jesus told people that their sins against others were forgiven. This makes sense only if He really was God incarnate.

Next Lewis treated what he called the "really foolish thing" some people say about Jesus: I accept Him as a great moral teacher but not His claim to be God. If He said these kinds of things and was not God, then He was certainly not a great moral teacher. Lewis made his famous statement: "He would either be a lunatic—on a level with the man who says he is a poached egg—or else he would be the Devil of Hell." Son of God, madman, or worse! Jesus did not leave it open to us to "come with any patronising nonsense about Him being a great human teacher." Either He is infinitely more or infinitely less! You must choose! (p. 56).

 COMMENTARY

This business of "self" is a tricky one indeed. In a real sense, all of human history can be divided into two camps with their different values or "loves." The inhabitants of these two camps—or cities—have two distinct views of morality. In the one, the principle of morality is love of God. In the other, the essence of evil, is selfishness (Phil. 3:17–4:1). Thus the human race can be divided into "two great camps," that of people who love the Lord and prefer God to self and that of people who prefer self to God.

CHAPTER 4: THE PERFECT PENITENT

Chapter at a Glance

The central Christian belief is that Jesus in dying put us right with God and gave us a new start. But how is this possible? Lewis developed carefully the doctrine of repentance and his understanding of the Christian doctrine of atonement. Only Jesus, the Christ, God incarnate, can be the perfect penitent.

Summary

Remember the options, the "frightening alternative," with which we are faced: this man is either who He said He was, a lunatic, or the devil. Lewis thought it was obvious that He was not a lunatic or a fiend. Our only logical choice is that God invaded our enemy-occupied world and He did so as a human. The purpose for all this? To teach, of course, but in the final analysis for something even more, far more, important—to die and to come to life again! This is what Christians think is the "chief point" of history, of His story.

Before he accepted Christ, Lewis was under the impression that the first point of Christian belief was that God wanted to punish us for having deserted Him and joining Satan. But Jesus "volunteered" for the punishment, and God "let us off." But Lewis maintained this theory is not Christianity. At the center of all Christian doctrine is that Jesus' death "put us right" and gives us a "fresh start" with the Father. Lewis said that

"Join with others in following my example, brothers, and take note of those who live according to the pattern we gave you. For, as I have often told you before and now say again even with tears, many live as enemies of the cross of Christ. Their destiny is destruction, their god is their stomach, and their glory is in their shame. Their mind is on earthly things. But our citizenship is in heaven. And we eagerly await a Savior from there, the Lord Jesus Christ, who by the power that enables him to bring everything under his control, will transform our lowly bodies so that they will be like his glorious body. Therefore, . . . stand firm in the Lord" (Phil. 3:17–4:1).

there are many theories about how this works but all Christians agree that it does work. We can accept Jesus as Savior and Lord without knowing exactly how. In fact, how could a person really be expected to know, to understand how all this works, until he has experienced it.

According to Lewis the "formula" that is Christianity is this: Jesus was killed for us; His death cleansed *our* sins; and through His death He conquered death itself. Theories as to how Jesus' death did this are secondary to the actual fact the theories are trying to explain. Some theories as to how this worked are worth considering.

Most people are familiar with the one Lewis has already mentioned. We are "let off" because Jesus, of His own free will, agreed to carry the punishment. Lewis believed that even on the surface this was a "very silly theory." If God was ready to let us off, why didn't He just do so? How does it make any sense to punish an innocent person instead? None, said Lewis, if by punishment we mean in the "police-court sense." But if we think in terms of a debt, we can understand how someone who has resources can pay a debt for someone who has none.

Fallen man is not just imperfect, needing improvement; he is a rebel who must surrender his weapons. It is not that man is only a little less than he should be but that he actively and intentionally rebelled against his very best, what he was intended to be. The only way out of his hole is surrender, what Christianity means by *repentance*. Repentance is no fun, said Lewis. It is much harder than "eating humble pie." It involves a great amount of unlearning—undoing the self-conceit and self-will humanity has been trained with for many thousands of years. It actually means to kill part of ourselves.

Now, proclaimed Lewis, comes the hitch: A man needs to be good to repent. The bad man needs repentance, but only a good one can repent perfectly. The more evil a man is, the more he needs repentance, yet the less he is able to repent. It turns out the only person who could do so faultlessly would be a perfect person. And, of course, such a person wouldn't need to repent!

This repentance is really a description of what going back to God is like. It is not so much what God demands as it is what we must do to get back to Him and our true, intended self. But because we have become bad and need repentance, this badness disables us, keeps us from doing what we should do. God must help us. Think for a minute: What if God became a man? What if human nature, which knows suffering and death, could be combined with divine nature in one person. Such an individual could help us, could surrender His will, suffer, and die, because He was man. He could also do it absolutely because He was God. Only if God did this for us could we go through this, and God could only do so as a man.

We must die to self, but we can only do so if God dies for us, and He can only die if He is a man. This is what Christians call the doctrine of the atonement. Lewis cautioned us to remember that he is only giving us a picture, not to be confused for the thing itself. If his picture is of no help, we should drop it.

Repentance—From the Greek *metanoia*, "a change of mind," and the Latin *re*, "again" and *poenitere*, "to make repent." In general usage, repentance is a feeling of sorrow for what one has done. In the New Testament, however, it means to turn away from sin and turn toward God and His will. Repentance radically transforms attitude and direction (see Matt. 4:17; Luke 1:16; 24:47; Acts 2:38; 3:19; 9:35; 11:21; 14:15; 15:19; 26:18–21; 1 Thess. 1:9; 1 Pet. 2:25).

Atonement—That aspect of the work of Christ, particularly His death, that makes possible the restoration of fellowship between God and man. The need for reconciliation between God and humankind is clear from the fact that people are sinners separated from God (Rom. 3:9–23). The doctrine of the atonement states that Christ died, or "atoned," for our sins, making reconciliation with God the Father possible. Atonement is effective because Christ bore the punishment justly due all sinners. Christ's dying on behalf of sinners is known as "vicarious" or "substitutionary" atonement.

COMMENTARY

This idea of God's dying to pay the debt which we on our own could not pay is the atonement, the wonderful scheme of redemption, which the Father put into place before the foundation of the world. This, wrote Lewis, is at the heart of Christianity because Jesus' death puts us right with God and gives a new chance with God, the Father. Jesus not only cleansed our sins but also conquered death for all who accept Him as Savior and Lord.

CHAPTER 5: THE PRACTICAL CONCLUSION

Chapter at a Glance

Chapter 5 reminds us of why Christ's could be the perfect surrender and humiliation. But what spreads this new life? Baptism, belief, and the Lord's Supper or Communion. These were taught on the authority of Jesus. These three do not take away our need to live for Him. Christians are in a different position because they have the Christ-life in them and thus can repent when they stumble. Christians have the responsibility to spread this life to the outside. God delayed His landing in force to give us a chance to accept Him before it is too late. Now may be the only chance we have!

Summary

As God, Jesus provided the example of perfection; as man, He provided the example of surrender and humiliation. Christian belief is that we must share in this humility and suffering, and if we do, we will share in His victory over death and have a new life in Him. This is far more than just trying to follow His teaching. The question is, How do we share in this new life?

Three things, according to Lewis, spread this new life in Christ to us: baptism, belief, and the Lord's Supper or Communion. These are the "ordinary methods." But Lewis was not saying there may not be special cases where new life is received without one or more of the three. He was also not going to talk about which of the three is most essential. Jesus taught His followers that new life was shared in this way. Lewis believed in Christ's authority, and we should not fear the word *authority*. Most of what we believe, 99 percent, is believed on authority.

Another "possible objection": Why didn't God land in force, instead of in enemy-occupied territory in "disguise" as it were? Why not act in force instead of starting a "secret society" to defeat Satan? He acted thus, Christians think, to give us a chance to freely join His side. But one day He will come in force. The people who raise this objection do not realize what they are saying. It will do no good, after God has landed in force, to say we are on His side. It will be much too late to choose sides then!

COMMENTARY

There is no question as to where Lewis would fall in the "modern" debate over the lordship of Christ. When we accept Jesus as Savior, we also accept Him as Lord of our lives. We *should* be taught that accepting Jesus as Savior and Lord involves growing in our understanding of what it means to accept Him as Lord and growing in actual Christian maturity. As Lewis wrote, baptism, belief, and the Lord's Supper

"Now, today, this moment, is our chance to choose the right side. God is holding back to give us that chance. It will not last for ever" (p. 66).

Lord—From the Anglo-Saxon *hlaford*, "bread keeper," one who has power or authority over others. The term often translated the Old Testament term *Yahweh* (Jehovah) and thus is used as a name for God. Christians also use the term as a name for Christ, God the Son (Phil. 2:11). Paul said in 1 Corinthians 8:6 that there is only "one Lord, Jesus Christ, through whom are all things, and we exist through Him" (see John 20:28; Acts 2:36; Rom. 5:11; 14:8; 1 Cor. 12:3; 16:22).

don't replace our need to "copy Christ," to grow in Christian living.

Lewis believed that we have a serious responsibility to care for this new life. And, again, we are back to repentance. In fact, you will find in the New Testament that the word *repentance* or the need to *repent* is used often of Christians. Remember the old bumper sticker: "Christians aren't perfect. They are just forgiven."

BOOK III: CHRISTIAN BEHAVIOUR

Book at a Glance

Book III contains twelve chapters which consider questions related to Christian morals. The first two chapters discuss the three parts of morality—with others, internal matters, and man with God; and the "cardinal virtues"—prudence, temperance, justice, and fortitude. Chapters 3 and 4 treat social morality and psychoanalysis. Chapters 5 and 6 are on sexual morality and Christian marriage. Chapters 7 and 8 deal with forgiveness and the "Great Sin." The last four chapters address charity, hope, and two on faith.

CHAPTER 1: THE THREE PARTS OF MORALITY

Chapter at a Glance

While human beings can go wrong in two ways—in relationship with others and what we are inside—there are really three parts to morality: relations with other human beings, our internal moral health, and how humanity relates to God.

Summary

The chapter starts with the story of a little boy who was asked what God was like. Through the boy we get the picture of morality as God running around snooping and trying to stop people from enjoying themselves. But, in the Christian sense, morality is to keep us from breaking down, straining, or having friction in running our "machine." Its purpose is to help us, not hinder us.

Christian perfection—At several points the Bible commands perfection of the believer: "Therefore you are to be perfect, as your heavenly Father is perfect" (Matt. 5:48 NASB; see also Matt. 19:21; Eph. 4:13–14; Heb. 13:21). But what is perfection? Groups in Christian history have suggested different answers. In Gnostic Christianity, perfection was the soul's release from the bondage of the flesh, a release attained thorough esoteric knowledge and illumination. In Pelagianism, perfection was the culmination of vigorous moral education and discipline. Still other movements have defined *perfection* as a mystical experience or a manifestation of ecstatic gifts of the Holy Spirit.

Church tradition since Augustine (354–430), however, has pictured perfection as perfect love, labeling it an impossibility in this life, except for saints. The Protestant Reformers went even further, saying perfection was possible for no one.

Thinking about morality *must* involve three spheres of duty: how we act person to person, what each of us is like inside, and how humankind relates to God, the Power who made us. Lewis thought everyone could work together in the first. Disagreements really start in the second. But it is in the third sphere that Christianity really differs from non-Christian morality. In the remainder of the book, he will "assume" the Christian position and look at the big picture from the Christian perspective.

COMMENTARY

Lewis hit the proverbial nail on its head here! Morality for the Christian is not something which hinders us but which frees us to be what we were really intended to be. As Christians, we are free at last to strive to live as God intended us to live with one another.

CHAPTER 2: THE "CARDINAL VIRTUES"

Chapter at a Glance

The "cardinal virtues"—prudence, temperance, justice and fortitude—are part of an older way of dividing up morality. Prudence is practical common sense, thinking about actions and the likely results. Temperance, or moderation, is "going the right length and no further." Justice is the old name for what we call "fairness": honesty, give-and-take, truthfulness, and promise keeping. Fortitude includes two kinds of courage.

Summary

The last chapter was structured with three parts to morality because it was originally composed as a ten-minute radio address in which brevity was needed. Here Lewis wanted to treat an older

How can we live out the very character of God with one another? Suggest examples: within the family, the church, at work, in our communities.

"With what shall I come before the LORD and bow down before the exalted God? Shall I come before him with burnt offerings, with calves a year old? Will the LORD be pleased with thousands of rams, with ten thousand rivers of oil? Shall I offer my firstborn for my transgression, the fruit of my body for the sin of my soul? He has showed you, O man, what is good. And what does the Lord require of you? To act justly and to love mercy and to walk humbly with your God" (Mic. 6:6–8).

way of dividing the subject matter. In this older view there were seven virtues. In Greek philosophy there were originally four. These Lewis discussed in this chapter—prudence, temperance, justice, and fortitude.

These virtues are referred to as "cardinal" because the Latin word means "the hinge of a door" or because they are "pivotal."

Prudence is defined as "practical common sense," thinking about what you are doing and the likely consequences. Today, Lewis said, people don't often think of prudence as one of the "virtues." Even many Christians think Jesus was saying we could only get into "His world" by being like little children and that all this means is by being good. They think this is enough. But Lewis pointed out that Jesus never meant for us to remain children "in *intelligence.*" We are to have a "child's heart, but a grown-up's head."

The meaning of the word *temperance* has changed. Originally it did not refer to total abstinence from alcohol or even abstaining. Originally it meant moderation, "going the right length and no further." Lewis listed three reasons an individual Christian may want to abstain from "strong drink" at a particular time: (1) This individual cannot handle his drinking. (2) He wants to use the money for the poor. (3) He is with people "inclined to drunkenness" and should not "encourage them" by his drinking.

Justice is really an old name for "fairness." It embraces honesty, give-and-take, truthfulness, keeping promises, and related things. *Fortitude* includes two types of courage: the type which faces danger and the kind that is strong under

Cardinal virtues—From the Latin *virtus* meaning "strength, courage." The highest virtues on which all others depend. Greek philosophy, some trace them to Plato, listed four basic or cardinal virtues: wisdom (prudence), courage (fortitude), justice (righteousness), and moderation (temperance). Christian teaching adds theological virtues—faith, hope, and love, as in 1 Corinthians 13:13—and together these form the seven cardinal virtues. The New Testament gives several lists of virtuous qualities: 1 Corinthians 13; Galatians 5:22–23; Philippians 4:8; Colossians 3:12–16 (see also 1 Thess. 1:3; Gal. 5:5–6; Col. 1:4–5; 2 Pet. 1:3–5; Eph.2:8–10)—Miethe, *The Compact Dictionary,* 54–55, 218.

"As Jesus started on his way, a man ran up to him and fell on his knees before him. 'Good teacher,' he asked, 'what must I do to inherit eternal life?' 'Why do you call me good?' Jesus answered. 'No one is good—except God alone. You know the commandments: "Do not murder, do not commit adultery, do not steal, do not give false testimony, do not defraud, honor your father and mother."' 'Teacher,' he declared, 'all these I have kept since I was a boy.' Jesus looked at him and loved him. 'One thing you lack,' he said. 'Go, sell everything you have and give to the poor, and you will have treasure in heaven. Then come, follow me.' At this the man's face fell. He went away sad, because he had great wealth" (Mark 10:17–22; see also Matt. 19:16–30; Luke 18:18–30).

pain. Lewis believed that practicing any other of the virtues for any length of time usually brings fortitude to the foreground.

This distinction between a "virtuous action" and being "virtuous" is important because, if we confuse the first with the second, we might be supporting three wrong ideas: (1) That doing the right thing was all that matters, not how or why we did it. Right behavior done for bad reasons won't help build internal character, and this is what matters in the end.

(2) People might think that God only wants obedience to rules. Far from this simplicity, He wants a particular sort of person. (3) People might think the virtues are essential only for physical life on earth. There might not be occasion for, say, just acts in heaven. But getting to be a certain kind of person is occasioned by doing just acts here. It is here on earth that we must become this sort of person, for it is too late after. The point is not that God will not admit us if we don't have "certain qualities of character," but unless we have "the beginnings of those qualities inside," then heaven—that deep, strong, unshakable happiness God wants for us—is not possible.

 COMMENTARY

Here we see that practical common sense, moderation, fairness (honesty, give-and-take, truthfulness, promise keeping), and courage are virtues important to the Christian life. They were considered important virtues in Greek and Roman Philosophy; e.g., the Roman emperor, Marcus Aurelius Antoninus (A.D. 121–180) said that his grandfather taught him "good morals" and how to control his temper. By his father, he was taught "modesty and manly character." His mother taught him "piety and beneficence" and abstinence from evil deeds and thoughts as well as simple living "far removed from the habits of the rich." His governor taught him "not to meddle with other people's affairs, and not to be ready to listen to slander." Certainly good lessons for any Christian, or any person, as well!

"He called a little child and had him stand among them. And he said: 'I tell you the truth, unless you change and become like little children, you will never enter the kingdom of heaven. Therefore, whoever humbles himself like this child is the greatest in the kingdom of heaven'" (Matt. 18:2–4).

CHAPTER 3: SOCIAL MORALITY

Chapter at a Glance

In the realm of social morality, Jesus didn't bring any really new-fashioned morality. The Golden Rule, "Do unto others as you would have them do unto you," really sums up what everyone knows is right. When we talk about Christian society, we need Christian educators, economists, and statesmen to lead. What is a fully Christian society like? There would be no passengers or parasites, but all would be workers. Lewis mentioned that the ancient Greeks, Jews, and Christians all agreed not to lend money at interest. Charity—giving to the poor—is essential to Christian morality.

Summary

The first thing, wrote Lewis, to be clear about Christian morality in the social sense—man to man—is that Jesus didn't come to present any brand new ethic. The Golden Rule in the New Testament sums up what everyone had always known to be correct behavior.

Second, Christianity does not intend a minute political agenda for applying the Golden Rule to a specific society at a particular instant. Rather, because it was meant for all at all times, it gives us general principles we must apply in particular situations. We are told to feed the hungry; however, we aren't given cooking lessons. We are told to read and study the Scriptures, but no automatic instruction in the biblical languages is suggested. But we do have, in the realm of the traditional arts and sciences, the resources available to learn to do a particular job. Christianity is like a "director" who shows us the right jobs and a "source of energy" from our new life; but we must respond, seek, and learn.

"He who has been stealing must steal no longer, but must work, doing something useful with his own hands, that he may have something to share with those in need" (Eph. 4:28; see also Luke 3:11 and 1 Thess. 4:11–12).

The ancient Greeks, the Old Testament Jews, and Christian teachers in the Middle Ages told us not to lend money at interest, Lewis reminded us. Advice completely ignored by the modern world; this very practice, called "investment," is the basis of our whole economic system. It may be that we are not totally wrong here, said Lewis. He will defer to the Christian economist, but he would have been dishonest had he not told us that "three great civilisations" all condemned the very practice on which we base our whole life.

The reason the New Testament declares that everyone must work is so we may have something to give to the poor! "Charity," giving to the poor, is an essential part of Christian morality. In the "frightening" parable of the sheep and the goats (Matt. 25:31–46), charity appears to be the detail on which "everything turns." However, Lewis didn't think we can settle how much to give. The only "safe rule" is that giving involves some sacrifice. If our spending on comforts, luxuries, and amusements is at the same level as others at our level of income, we are likely "giving way too little."

COMMENTARY

Lewis hammered home at least three important points in this chapter:

1. Lewis pointed to the priesthood of all believers, saying that Christians in all walks of life must integrate their beliefs with their actions, their faith with their work.

2. In reminding us of the three great societies' agreement in forbidding interest, or what they called "usury," Lewis unloaded a potential bomb. Christians today should seriously examine the "financial instruments" they participate in as a part of everyday life with regard to the faith and how wealth is to be distributed. For there can be no question that Christians are supposed to be a force in wealth distribution.

3. Another important point raised in this chapter was about the poor. Lewis believed that giving, to be real, must involve sacrifice.

CHAPTER 4: MORALITY AND PSYCHOANALYSIS

Chapter at a Glance

Both Christian morality and psychoanalysis claim to be techniques to put the "human machine right." Psychoanalysis, as such, is not contradictory to Christianity, but Freud's philosophy is.

Summary

To begin, two points are made: (1) Both Christian morality and psychoanalysis claim to be able to put the "human machine right," so we need to compare them. (2) Christian morality is really not about obeying lots of rules but is

Think seriously about the parable of the sheep and the goats. If, as is clearly taught, Christ makes the division between those who receive eternal life and eternal punishment based on how we responded to the needs of the hungry, the stranger, the needy, the sick, and those in prison; what are you and your church doing that show you are numbered among the sheep?

Sigmund Freud (1856–1940) studied medicine at the University of Vienna. He was the founder of the Psychoanalytic School and is considered by some to be the father of modern psychology. He became interested in the treatment of neuroses and went to Paris in 1885 to study. He used hypnotic methods in combination with his own techniques of free association and dream interpretation. He developed complex psychological theory of which the main tenets are the predominance of sex and the doctrine of the subconscious.

about becoming a different kind of person by making and reinforcing certain choices.

We must distinguish clearly between the actual medical theories and techniques of psychoanalysts and the philosophical worldview that Freud and others held. Clearly Freud's philosophy is in direct contradiction to Christianity. Lewis said that when Freud spoke about curing neurotics it was his field of specialty, but when he spoke about general philosophy he was only an amateur.

Psychoanalysis itself is not at all contradictory to Christianity. Ultimately the two are doing different things. Both are concerned with choice of which there are two components: (1) the act of choosing, and (2) various feelings and impulses with which "his psychological outfit" gives him the "raw material" of his choice. This raw material is either "normal"—feelings common to all people or "unnatural"—a result of things "gone wrong" in the subconscious. Several examples are given: Fear of really dangerous things is normal. Fear of cats or spiders is irrational. A man desiring a woman is natural, but man desiring man is not.

Psychoanalysis may cure subconscious, irrational fears which "no amount of moral effort" can help. Morality, however, is only concerned with free choice. "Bad psychological material" is a disease not a sin. A disease needs to be cured. Sin needs to be repented. This is most important. Humans judge one another by their external actions. God judges us by our moral choices. Humans see the results of choices. God judges not on the raw material but on what we do with it.

Lewis's second point was this: Christian morality is making the right choices with the result being a change of character. In our choices we are slowly turning our inner self into either a "heavenly" or a "hellish" creature.

Finally, Lewis asked us to remember that the right direction leads not only to peace but also to knowledge. As we get better, we understand more and more clearly the evil still in us. Conversely, as a man gets worse, he understands his "badness less and less." When we are "moderately bad," we know we have problems, but a "thoroughly bad" individual thinks he is fine. Actually, common sense tells us: We understand sleep when awake, not when asleep. We know the nature of drunkenness when sober, not when drunk. Good people know both good and evil; bad ones know about neither!

COMMENTARY

Christians must be aware that a "general philosophical view of the world" is always behind—beneath, foundational to—psychological theories. Every psychological theory has presuppositions about the nature of man and other beliefs. Christians, even those trained in psychology, must be careful that they both understand the biblical view of man and the presuppositions and assumptions regarding the nature of man behind a particular psychological theory or counseling technique. Lewis said in no uncertain terms that Freud's philosophy was definitely contradictory to Christianity.

With the challenges of modern-day life, how is your church preparing you for ministry/witness in this important time? How are you preparing?

CHAPTER 5: SEXUAL MORALITY

Chapter at a Glance

The virtue of chastity never changes, but the rule of propriety does. Chastity is the most unpopular

Lust—From the Greek *epithumia*, "strong desire of any kind"; *hedone*, "pleasure," "enjoyment"; *orego*, "to desire"; *orexis*, "longing"; *pathos*, "passion"; and the Latin *lascivus*, "wanton." Originally, *lust* meant only strong desire or craving for an object, pleasure, or delight. It did not have a negative or positive connotation. The word is used of a good desire in Luke 22:15; Philippians 1:23; and 1 Thessalonians 2:17. Today it is used negatively, as in Romans 6:12, where it refers to an evil desire, as it does in Romans 13:14; Galatians 5:16, 24; and Ephesians 2:3. In Roman Catholic theology, it is considered one of the seven deadly sins—Miethe, *The Compact Dictionary*, 132.

In a world where we are so constantly bombarded with sex and sexual images, what can we do not only to counter this effect but also to have a healthy attitude toward sex? Should the church be helping in this area? What can it do?

Christian virtue because our sexual instinct has become perverted. We are so constantly bombarded with sexual lies and half-truths that it is difficult to escape. We must want to be cured before we can be and then we will need God's help. Three reasons are given as to why it is now especially difficult for us to desire complete chastity. But the center of Christian morality is not found in sexual morality.

Summary

Here, we turn to what Christians refer to as the "virtue of chastity," or sexual morality. The rule of Christian chastity never changes, but the social rule of propriety, modesty, or decency does. Lewis gave the example of a Victorian lady covered with cloths head to foot and a Pacific islands girl wearing almost nothing. Both are equally modest, proper, or decent by the standard of each respective society; and both could be equally virtuous. But, when one breaks the rule of propriety in their society to "excite lust," he or she offends against chastity.

Chastity is the most unpopular Christian virtue. The "old Christian rule" is complete faithfulness in marriage or total abstinence. Yet this seems in our day "so contrary to our instincts." Lewis said this is because our sexual instinct has gone wrong.

Though Lewis spoke at length about sex, he wanted to make clear that the heart of Christian morality is not found here. It is not the supreme vice for Christianity. In fact, he said that the sins of the flesh are the least bad of all sins. This is because the worst pleasures are purely spiritual—placing others in the wrong, bossing, patronizing, backbiting, power, hatred. The "Diabolical self" is much worse than the "Animal self." Hence, a "cold, self-righteous" churchgoing "prig" may be closer to hell than a prostitute. But, of course, it is much better to be neither one.

Each individual has the God-given right and *responsibility* to judge himself or herself with regard to personal integrity. Christ *alone*—not self-righteous coworkers, nosy neighbors, or religious bigots—has the right to judge.

COMMENTARY

The rule of Christian chastity *never* changes, but social rules of modesty or decency do change. Thus, motive is important in this discussion.

Mere Christianity was written in the mid-1940s, so Lewis was claiming that this unhealthy situation regarding sex had been going on since the 20s. But if he thought people had been "fed all day long on good solid lies" about sex then, just think about how much more we are thus fed today! *Everything* is sold using sex—garden tractors, gasoline, alcohol, and food. Youth today are actually, really forcefully, bombarded with sex and sexual messages everywhere they turn! But we must also remember that the heart of Christian morality is not found here!

CHAPTER 6: CHRISTIAN MARRIAGE

Chapter at a Glance

Christian marriage is the proper place for sex. Christ's words tell us that in Christian marriage the two become a single organism. How can a single organism not be for the duration, for life? The relationship of the Christian virtue justice, promise keeping, and love and marriage is discussed. Love, as distinct from "being in love" is not merely a feeling, but a deep unity, maintained by will, strengthened by habit. Our idea of love from books, movies, and plays is not the Christian one. In another way Christian marriage is different from generally held social

"'Haven't you read,' he replied, 'that at the beginning the Creator "made them male and female," and said, "For this reason a man will leave his father and mother and be united to his wife, and the two will become one flesh"? So they are no longer two, but one. Therefore what God has joined together, let man not separate'" (Matt. 19:4–6; see also Mark 10:5–9).

The Bible teaches that God intended marriage to be for life, so what can the church do to help get this important truth across? Should the church be the place where people who have just a casual relationship, or no relationship at all with the church, come to be married?

beliefs: God has given the man the responsibility of being the head of this union.

Summary

For two reasons Lewis didn't want to deal with Christian marriage: The Christian doctrines on this subject are (1) extremely unpopular. And when he was writing *Mere Christianity*, he had (2) never been married.

Christian marriage is based on Jesus' words that a man and woman are one flesh—in modern English, a "single organism." This is a *fact* just as a lock and a key are one mechanism.

Christ, who created us, was telling us that a male, one "half," and a female, the other "half," were meant to be combined in pairs. This paring was not meant to be just physical, but a total paring! The "monstrosity," said Lewis, of having sex outside marriage is that in so doing we are trying to isolate sexual union from all other kinds which were intended to go with it to make a total union.

Because of the intent of this total union, Christianity teaches that marriage is for life! Though there are different views regarding whether or when divorce is permissible in different churches, all agree that divorce is not a "simple readjustment of partners." Divorce is like a surgery that dismembers a living body.

Before looking at the modern view with regard to marriage, we are reminded of the virtue of justice which includes promise keeping. Of course, when we were married in a church, we made a "public, solemn promise" to stay together until death. This was a promise made before and to God! Lewis argued that if the sexual impulse *is* just like all other impulses, as moderns say, then treat it as such! Other impulses, other indulgences, are controlled by our promises, and so should our sexual impulse!

The chapter ends with a discussion of something "even more unpopular" than the idea that marriage should be permanent: Christian wives promise to obey the husband. Lewis said this raises two questions: Why the need for a head at all? Why should the man be it? As long as the two partners agree, there is no need for a "head." He hoped this is the normal state in a Christian marriage. But what if there is real disagreement? First, talk it over seriously. But if agreement cannot be reached and if marriage is to be permanent, one of the two must have the "power of deciding."

Why the man? Lewis said there must be something unnatural about wives ruling over husbands, "because the wives themselves are half ashamed of it and despise the husbands whom they rule." Another reason is given which comes from Lewis's observation as a bachelor. The family's "foreign policy" must depend on the man. "A woman is primarily fighting for her own children and husband against the rest of the world" (p. 103).

Lewis pointed out some important truths about love here. What can we do to understand the difference between "being in love" and the "thrill" of love, and how can we instill this important truth in our children, families, and churches?

COMMENTARY

Love is not just an emotion, nor should it be. Commitment does not come out of love, but love should come out of commitment. Commitment and promise keeping are what love is all about. The fact that we think the other way round is evidence that our idea of love has been perverted! Love involves so much more than

"Love is patient, love is kind. It does not envy, it does not boast, it is not proud. It is not rude, it is not self-seeking, it is not easily angered, it keeps no record of wrongs. Love does not delight in evil but rejoices with the truth. It always protects, always trusts, always hopes, always perseveres. Love never fails" (1 Cor. 13:4–8).

There is no substitute for communication in a strong, lasting marriage. Demands on time today sometimes limit couples' conversation. How can a couple create time to talk and really continue to know each other? How can the church help with this?

sex and sexuality. Love involves respect, appreciation, admiration. Marriage is the most sacred bond and wonderful relationship two persons can share. Through it they become one in the eyes of God!

CHAPTER 7: FORGIVENESS

Chapter at a Glance

The Christian virtue of forgiveness is a hard one, but it is at the center of the faith. It means forgiving even our enemies. It doesn't mean liking them but loving them as we love ourselves.

Summary

This chapter is about a Christian virtue perhaps more unpopular than chastity. "Love your neighbor as yourself " (Matt. 22:39) may be even more unpopular because "neighbor" includes your enemy. Thus, we have "come up against" the "terrible duty" of forgiving even enemies. Everyone says that forgiveness is a "lovely idea"; that is, until the need to do it actually becomes a reality. Of course, Lewis was thinking of what had just happened in World War II. Then people thought charity was a virtue too high or difficult. Lewis was not trying to tell us what he would do but what Christianity is.

Right in the middle of Christianity is "forgive us our sins as we also forgive everyone who sins against us" (Luke 11:4). Jesus says that we will not be forgiven if forgiveness is not in us. This is hard, no question about it. But two things can be done which might make it easier: (1) Start with something easier, something short of the "Gestapo." (2) Try to understand exactly what loving your neighbor as yourself really means.

Loving your neighbor doesn't mean being fond of them, being attracted to them, or thinking them nice. As Christians, we are to hate the corrupt actions of a bad man but not the man. Hate the sin not the sinner. For years Lewis thought this silly but finally realized that there was, in fact, one person to whom he had been doing this all along: himself! There were many traits he did not like in himself, may have even loathed, but he still loved himself.

COMMENTARY

Lewis said that everyone thinks forgiveness is a "lovely idea" until they need to forgive! The doctrine of forgiveness is right at the heart of Christianity. God first had to forgive us for there to be any possibility of a real relationship with Him! And, because He forgave us, we must forgive others if we are to be forgiven.

One of the worst things in the world today is an institutional church that does not teach the reality and assurance of forgiveness. But what is truly even worse is other Christians who because of their legalistic bigotry won't allow it! What can you do to express, and what is your church doing to teach, the reality of God's forgiveness and make it real in the lives of believers?

CHAPTER 8: THE GREAT SIN

Chapter at a Glance

The "great sin" is none other than the sin of pride or self-conceit, the opposite of Christian humility. It is at the root of all vices and all sin.

Summary

This is the part of Christian morals most sharply different from other moral systems. There is one vice *everyone* has, yet everybody loathes in others. Lewis had never heard anyone who is not a Christian "accuse himself" of this defect. No fault makes a person more unpopular, and yet there is no fault of which we are more unconscious. The more we are guilty of it, the more we hate it in others. What is it? Pride or self-conceit.

Pride—The exact opposite of humility. It consists of excessive love of self and is exhibited in three ways: (1) contempt for lawful authority; (2) contempt for equals and inferiors; and (3) desire to surpass one's equals. In Roman Catholic theology pride is one of the seven deadly sins. Thomas Aquinas put pride in a class by itself as the most deadly and devastating of all vices, because it is part of every sin. Certainly the Bible warns against false pride (see Prov. 8:13; 11:2; 16:18; 1 John 2:16; Mark 7:22; James 4:16)—Miethe, *The Compact Dictionary*, 165.

In Christian morality, its opposite is called humility. When talking about sexual morality, Lewis warned that the heart of Christian morality was not in this. The "essential vice," the "utmost evil," is none other than pride. All the other vices are "mere fleabites" when compared to this one. This was the sin of Satan, and according to Augustine, the root of all sin.

A test to find out how much pride you have is to see just how much you dislike it in others. Our pride is in serious rivalry with everyone else's pride. Lewis said we must be clear that pride is in essence competitive. The real pleasure of pride is not in having something but in having more of it than another.

Lewis wanted to "guard against" possible misunderstandings here: The pleasure we may feel from, or when someone else praises us for, doing something right, or for someone else is not pride. There is a vast difference between thinking it good to have pleased another and thinking "what a fine person I am" to have done this or that. The vain person does things to get praise, applause, and admiration. This is a "childlike" fault. Real "black, diabolical" pride is when we disdain others so much that we don't care what they think of us. On the other hand, it is right—our duty—not to care what others think of us. We are to care infinitely more what God thinks.

To have a warmhearted respect for, as when saying we are "proud" of a son or grandson, is not the sin of pride. It depends entirely on what we do with the "feeling." If we "put on airs" because we have a "distinguished father," then it would be a fault, but still better than pride simply in oneself.

We must not think that God forbids pride, being offended at it, or wants humility because He Himself is proud. No, the point is that He wants us to know Him. He wants to give Himself to us. God is such that to get in touch with Him we will be "delightedly humble."

A truly humble person probably won't be what most call "humble." "He will not be a sort of greasy, smarmy person, who is always telling you that, of course, he is nobody. Probably all you will think about him is that he seemed a cheerful, intelligent chap who took a real interest in what *you* said to *him*." The very first step—a big one—in acquiring humility is to realize that you are proud. Thinking that you are not conceited is to be "very conceited indeed."

 COMMENTARY

Pride is so extreme a sin that it is the reason we pit ourselves against God! It is the reason we dare think we can be gods! Augustine thought it the root of all evil. Aquinas believed it to be the most deadly and devastating of all vices, part of every sin. This is why Lewis said that as long as we suffer from pride we cannot know God.

Some years ago, a popular television mini-series entitled *The Thorn Birds* outraged many Roman Catholics because of how the priest, Father Ralph, was portrayed. But Father Andrew M. Greeley, a noted scholar and author said this about the "whole affair": "Father Ralph's worst sins are not of the flesh but of the spirit—ambition and insensitivity—sins that, curiously enough, are most unlikely to offend Catholic conservatives, who will howl shrilly about a priest's falling in love and having sex with a sheep rancher's daughter. Adultery for such folks is the most terrible of sins, indeed the only real sin. Pride, greed, heartlessness—they hardly matter."

What can we do, what can the church do, to help people see in a most positive way the true evil of sins of the spirit as the "root cause" of all other sin?

But pride is a ravaging spiritual cancer. It hides itself so well in all other sins. Pride often hides in the houses and communities we live in, the people we associate with, the cars we drive, and the way we use material things. Pride hides itself even better in "religious" attitudes like righteous indignation or spiritual superiority. But as long as Satan has succeeded in convincing us to switch the tables with regard to sins of the flesh and sins of the spirit, we will hardly even notice the real cancer.

CHAPTER 9: CHARITY

Chapter at a Glance
Charity is one of the theological virtues. In the Christian sense, *charity* means "love." Christian love, or charity, is not the same as liking or affection. Though Christian charity is distinct from affection, it is something we do because God loves everyone as He loves us; it does lead to affection.

Summary
Charity was treated partly with regard to forgiveness. Here Lewis wanted to add a little more. Charity, once called "alms," had a much broader meaning. In the Christian sense, *charity* means love. But this love is not an emotion; it is a state of the will. Lewis alluded to what he said in chapter 7, that love does not mean we like ourselves or another. Rather, it means we desire our own good or the good of another. Though it is natural to feel charitable toward people we

like or for whom we have affection, it can also be a wrong thing. Lewis gave the example of a "doting mother" who may spoil her child. What this is really doing is gratifying the mother's tender tendencies at the expense of the child's real happiness as he or she gets older. But charity is about much more than "affectionate feelings."

Lewis encourages us not to worry about whether we love our neighbors but to act as if we did. This is one of the "great secrets"! For when we act *as if* we love someone, we will find soon that we do. The exception is, of course, if we do a favor for another so they will see what a wonderful person we are and wait for gratitude, we will be disappointed most likely. But when we do something good for another simply because God also made that other person, we may learn to love him or her. The difference between a "worldly man" and a Christian is that the first treats people he likes kindly whereas the Christian treats everyone kindly—and ends up liking more people.

"The smallest good act today is the capture of a strategic point from which, a few months later, you may be able to go on to victories you never dreamed of" (p. 117).

Lewis thought that both good and evil grow "at compound interest." This is a good reason the daily little decisions are of infinite importance. Some writers use *charity,* not just for man's love for his fellow but also to describe God's love for man and visa versa. What we must remember is that, though our feelings come and go, God's love for us is steadfast. He is not "wearied" by our sin and wants us to be "cured" at any cost to us or to Him.

If giving is one of *the* signs of a regenerated heart, how can we better understand this and implement it? How can the church help?

COMMENTARY

Giving is one of *the* signs of a regenerated heart! Christians must give alms, or do works of char-

Hope—The belief that God will keep His promises for the future. We base this hope on the evidence of His faithfulness in the past. Hope includes confidence in all Christian promises not yet a reality in the life of a believer. Certainly, belief in life after death and an eternity in heaven is important. In 1 Corinthians 15:19 (NASB), Paul said: "If we have hoped in Christ in this life only, we are of all men most to be pitied."

Christians should be able to defend their hope: In 1 Peter 3:15 (NASB), the Christian is told to "sanctify Christ as Lord in your hearts, always being ready to make a defense to everyone who asks you to give an account for the hope that is in you, yet with gentleness and reverence." In 1 Peter 3:15, the word *"heart"* refers to the center of our being, our minds. We are told to be able to give a defense of our hope in the gospel because of the evidence for the truth of Christianity —Miethe, *The Compact Dictionary*, 109.

ity, simply because it is the right thing to do. But the remarkable thing about acts of giving and doing acts of kindness is that they not only make the doers feel better, but they also enable them to be better in the future! Lewis rightly noted that both good and evil grow at compound interest.

"Love" is a state of the will. But what is the "will"? For starters, it takes willpower to make a dream come true! But what is willpower? Only man, as a rational animal, possesses will. The word *volition* means "to will." Will is the ability of human self-determination. Human will is the strongest possible assent, rational determination, to accomplish no matter what. It is more than just intellect or appetite.

CHAPTER 10: HOPE

Chapter at a Glance
Hope is the continual looking forward to heavenly bliss. There are many reasons we have difficulty wanting heaven. Our whole education teaches us to zero in on this world; therefore, we often don't recognize our real desire for heaven.

Summary
Hope is the second of the theological virtues Lewis treated. Looking forward to eternity in heaven is not escapism but something Christians are meant to do. In history, you will find that the Christians who did the most for our present world were the ones who thought most about the next. Lewis gave several examples: the apostles, the great Christians of the Middle Ages, and English Evangelicals who helped stop the slave trade.

Further, because we Christians have stopped thinking of heaven, we have become "ineffec tive" in this world. "Aim at Heaven and you will get earth 'thrown in': aim at earth and you will get neither" (p. 118). Lewis said that most of us have difficulty wanting heaven, (1) because our whole instruction is inclined to attach our minds to this world, and (2) sometimes we don't recognize the desire for heaven in us when we have it. If we really looked in our hearts, we would realize that what we truly want cannot be supplied by this world.

There are two wrong ways of addressing this reality and one correct one: (1) The fool blames the things themselves. He believes if he had married a different woman or vacationed in a different country, his longings would have been satisfied. (2) In "The Way of the Disillusioned Sensible Man," the child grows up and realizes he can't catch and shouldn't chase the rainbow. You settle down and don't expect too much. This is better than the first and would be the best way *if* man did not live forever.

The correct way is (3) the Christian way. We *are* born with desires. Many examples are given: Baby's feel hunger, and food exists to satisfy that desire. It follows that if we have a desire which this world cannot satisfy it is because we were made for another world. Earthly pleasures were only meant to arouse our heavenly desire, to suggest the real thing, not to satisfy it. If this is true, then "earthly blessings" are real, and we should be thankful for them but never mistake them for the real thing.

 ## COMMENTARY

Looking forward to eternity in heaven is far from being escapism. This hope is that which frees up the Christian to enjoy this life without being enslaved by it. Insightfully, Lewis pointed out that when, as Christians, we stop looking toward heaven we become impotent in this world. This view of heaven keeps us from being "one-eyed" in this world and thus loosing our peripheral vision or depth and perspective. Heaven puts the proper perspective to the world in which we live!

CHAPTER 11: FAITH

Chapter at a Glance
Chapter 11 is the first of two chapters on faith. This word is used by Christians on two levels. The first is simply belief, accepting Christian doctrines as true.

Summary
Faith is the third of the Christian virtues. It is used by Christians in two senses, on two levels. This chapter deals with the first sense, what Lewis called simply "belief," accepting the doctrines of Christianity as true. While this seems "fairly simple," non-Christians—and Lewis himself before he became a Christian—are puzzled as to why Christians think faith is a virtue. Lewis believed that a sane man accepts or rejects any statement because he thinks the evidence good or bad. If he is mistaken about the evidence, he is not a bad man but "merely stupid." So how is "faith" a virtue?

But Lewis was assuming that the mind was completely ruled by reason. Not so, he said. Even when the mind is convinced by good evidence and reason, imagination and emotion can affect it. Emotion and imagination can battle with faith and reason. So, for Lewis, faith is the art of gripping reasonably accepted things, even with changing moods. Thus, faith is a necessary vir-

Faith—From the Greek *pistis*, "firm persuasion." The word *faith* appears only 2 times in the Old Testament (Deut. 32:20 and Hab. 2:4). It appears 307 times in the New Testament. Biblical faith has two essential components: (1) trust or acceptance, belief that Jesus is Lord with acknowledgment of His resurrection, and (2) intellectual content, the revealed truth that is firmly believed and reflected in the life of the believer. The New Testament in no way teaches that we should have a blind faith. Even the aspect of trust in faith is not blind—Miethe, *The Compact Dictionary*, 90.

tue, and we "must train the habit of Faith," or we will never be a sound Christian.

Next Lewis turned to the second sense or higher level of faith. This is the most difficult thing he has attempted to this point. He went back to the subject of humility. The first step toward that virtue is to realize that we are proud. Now we are told that the next step is to make a serious attempt—say six weeks—to practice Christian virtues. We really cannot know how bad we are until we try hard to be good. We can only know how strong temptation really is when we try to resist. Thus, wrote Lewis, bad people know little about their disease, "badness." Jesus, the only man to resist temptation totally, is the only person who knows fully what temptation means. Jesus is the only total realist. Thus, the main thing learned by really attempting to practice Christian virtues is that we fail. Real Christianity blows to bits the idea that we can simply "perform" and be good Christians. Unfortunately, some then give up trying at all and give up their faith. If you "stick with it," you soon have "another discovery": God gives you everything you need to please Him. Christians are like the boy who goes to his father to ask for money to buy his father a present. When we realize these two things, God can really begin to work in us.

COMMENTARY

In many ways, the biblical doctrine of faith is the most central, foundational doctrine of all Christianity and yet the most misunderstood. The world *faith* appears only 2 times in the Old Testament (Deut. 32:20 and Hab. 2:4). It appears 307 times in the New Testament. When you consult a Greek dictionary for definitions of

"If any of you lacks wisdom, he should ask God, who gives generously to all without finding fault, and it will be given to him. But when he asks, he must believe and not doubt, because he who doubts is like a wave of the sea, blown and tossed by the wind. That man should not think he will receive anything from the Lord; he is a double-minded man, unstable in all he does" (James 1:5–8).

faith, you will find two essential aspects that penetrate to the heart of the biblical teaching: (1) trust or acceptance; belief that Jesus is Lord, with acknowledgment of His resurrection, and (2) intellectual content, the revealed truth that is firmly believed and is reflected in the life of the believer.

CHAPTER 12: FAITH

Chapter at a Glance

Some aspects of the Christian faith cannot be understood from outside; they can only be understood after having traveled down the road. Faith in the higher sense is when we realize that having tried hard to practice Christian virtues we fail. Then we realize that we are bankrupt. Only God can do what we need done. We must "leave it to God." But we must also act. The Bible puts faith and action together in one "amazing sentence": Philippians 2:12–13. In our better moments, we get a glimpse of the fact that Christianity is far more than morality, duty, rules, etc. It is about being in His presence!

Summary

Lewis began this chapter by telling us that if we don't understand what he says in this chapter to leave it alone. Some things in Christianity cannot be understood from outside but can only be understood after having gone a distance down the Christian road. Faith in the second sense or on the higher level comes only after a person has tried "his level best" to practice Christian virtues and has failed. He must realize that every good he does is really from God. He must discover that he is bankrupt.

What God really cares about is not so much actions but that we become people "of a certain kind of quality." When we are right with God, we will be right with our fellowmen. But we cannot get into a right relationship with God until we discover, really discover, that we are bankrupt. We have to try hard and fail before we can see this. This is when we will turn to God and say: "You must do this. I can't." But this might not happen suddenly. It may happen gradually. What is really important is the change itself, that we are no longer confident about our own efforts but know we must leave everything to God.

Leaving it to God for the Christian means to put all one's trust in Jesus, that Christ will remake us into "sonship," make us "Sons of God." In another sense, giving everything over to Jesus doesn't mean we stop trying. How can we say we trusted someone if we did not take his advice? Yes, we must try to obey Him, but in a new, less worried way. Doing certain things not to be good or to get into heaven but because He is in us already and we have a "first faint gleam of Heaven" inside.

"Good actions" and "Faith in Christ" are like the two blades of a pair of scissors. The scissors cannot cut without both! Christians have been accused of, on the one hand, believing that only good actions matter and, on the other, that only faith matters—that if one has faith it doesn't matter what one does. Both positions are nonsense.

"Therefore, my dear friends, as you have always obeyed—not only in my presence, but now much more in my absence—continue to work out your salvation with fear and trembling, for it is God that works in you to will and to act according to his good purpose. Do everything without complaining or arguing, so that you may become blameless and pure, children of God without fault in a crooked and depraved generation, in which you shine like stars in the universe as you hold out the word of life" (Phil. 2:12–16).

 **COMMENTARY**

Faith in the higher sense, according to Lewis, is when we realize after trying our best we cannot even practice Christianity on our own; we are

Faith is a conscious mental desire to do the will of the God of Scripture! Consider and apply this definition with regard to your life.

bankrupt. To become people of a certain kind of quality, we must turn our lives over to God. What is really important is not whether this happens suddenly or gradually but that it happens. We must come to the point where we seriously desire God, that we put all our trust in Jesus. We don't stop trying, but we do so with a new trust, assurance, and in a "less worried way."

Book at a Glance

Book IV contains eleven chapters which consider questions "Beyond Personality." These chapters are a discussion of the first steps in understanding the doctrine of the Trinity. Lewis had been warned not to include this material because the ordinary reader is not interested in theology. He rejected this idea because he didn't think the ordinary reader is such a fool.

Chapter 1 is about the difference between making and begetting. Chapter 2 is about the Trinity. Chapter 3 treats the issue of God's relation to what we experience as time. Chapter 4 is about being "infected" by Christ. Man, according to chapter 5, is like an "Obstinate Toy Soldier" who fights becoming the real person he was intended to be. Chapter 6 attempts to clear up two misunderstandings arising from chapter 5. Chapter 7 is about pretending, what it involves and who is doing it. Chapter 8 tells us that Christianity is both hard and easy and why both are true. Chapter 9 is about "Counting the Cost" involved when we accept Christ and allow Him to start the massive rebuilding process in us. Chapter 10 tells us that He intends for us to be new men, not just nice people. And chapter 11 discusses this new man.

CHAPTER 1: MAKING AND BEGETTING

Chapter at a Glance

Theology is practical. It is not the "thing in itself," but it is like a map which is important both to see perspective and to travel in understanding.

Summary

Theology is not as real as the God it tells us about. But the "map" is important in two ways: (1) It is based on what hundreds, thousands, of others have discovered is real. Theology, viewed as a map, fits all the different experiences together. (2) If a person wants to go anywhere, the map is "absolutely necessary." Certainly, doctrines aren't God, but they are a sort of map. In both of these senses, theology is actually practical. It also keeps us from being taken in by uninformed, or simply wrong, popular ideas of Christianity.

We are reminded that in one of the creeds Christ is said to be the "begotten, not created" Son of God who existed before the material world. This is not referring to the virgin birth at all. This is the claim that Christ existed before nature, before time. He was not created, but "begotten." Lewis asked what this means.

The words *begetting* or *begotten* aren't used much today. Yet everyone still knows their meaning. To *beget* means to be the father of, to bear something the same kind as yourself. Whereas, to create is simply to make. Thus, the first thing we must clarify is that what God begets is God. But what God creates is not God. This is why people are not the same as Christ when we talk of "Sons of God." People may be like God in certain ways, but we are not of the same nature as God.

Man in his natural condition does not have "spiritual life" which is a "higher and different sort of life" and exists in God. Lewis believed that the difference between "biological life" and "spiritual life" are so important that he gave them two distinct names. The first is "bios" because it needs to be "kept up by incessant subsidies" like air, water, and food. The second is "zoe," which refers to the spiritual life in God from all eternity. "bios" has a "shadowy" or "symbolic" similarity to "zoe."

 COMMENTARY

Theology is practical. It does help us fit all our different experiences together and understand the whole picture. But many Christians are almost afraid of theology, or even knowledge in general. Many people fear education. And certainly education can be misused. But we should fear its opposite far more! After all, the only way to combat the misuse of education is to know (John 8:32)! Theology *should* help us avoid being taken in by uninformed or wrong popular ideas about Christianity.

We should never understate the importance of knowledge to the Christian faith, for knowledge is at its very heart. The word *disciple* means a learner and a doer. We must know not only *what* we believe but *why*. Yet we must never forget that people don't care how much we know until they know how much we *care*! When they see our love, only then can the constant years of study, intellectual and spiritual preparation, be used to Christ's glory.

CHAPTER 2: THE THREE-PERSON GOD

Chapter at a Glance
God is beyond personality, but He is not impersonal. He is superpersonal. He is three persons in one being. This is why theology is practical. Theology helps us understand the complexity of truth.

Summary
Many people say they believe in God but not in a personal God, as if they think this "mysterious something" behind all must be more than a mere person. Christians agree. But to think of

God as "impersonal" is really to think of Him as something less than personal, not more. Christianity is the only religion which offers any idea of a deity who is "superpersonal." Only Christianity has any concept of how humans can be taken into the life of God and still remain themselves, actually much more themselves than before. Christians believe this is the whole reason we exist.

Lewis reminded us of the three dimensions of space: left or right, backward or forward, up or down—and what this means. A straight line is one dimension; a drawn figure is two dimensions; and a cube uses all three. The point is that, as we progress to the "more real" and also "more complicated" levels, we don't leave behind the things we found on the simpler ones. Rather, we use them in new combined ways that we couldn't have imagined if we knew only straight lines.

There are many important Scriptures regarding the Trinity, including Matthew 3:16; 28:19; John 10:30; 14:16; 1 Corinthians 12:4–6; 2 Corinthians 5:19; Ephesians 1:3–14; Philippians 2:6. Any teaching that denies the Trinity, such as Tritheism (belief in three separate gods) or Unitarianism (belief in God as one person alone), is considered heretical by Christianity.

The Christian concept of God involves the same principle. In God's level we will find personalities related in new ways we cannot imagine if we don't live on that level. Thus, in God's level, in His "dimension," we find a being who is three persons and yet one.

Certainly, if Christianity were just something made up, something easier could be conceived. But, because it is fact, we cannot compete "in simplicity" with those inventing systems of belief.

COMMENTARY

The doctrine of the Trinity is a good example of the importance of, and need for, theology.

The word *Trinity* never appears in the Bible, though the doctrine clearly does.

In the first centuries A.D., the early church worked out the implications of the clear teaching of Scripture with regard to the Trinity. The Nicene Creed (A.D. 325) teaches that all three members of the Trinity share in the divine essence, making them God.

Since the word *Trinity* does not appear in the Bible, why is the doctrine so important to Christians?

CHAPTER 3: TIME AND BEYOND TIME

Chapter at a Glance

The whole idea of time as we experience it and God's relationship to it is discussed in this chapter. Lewis suggested that God is not in time. This helps us understand problems which arise for some with regard to the Incarnation (how God can be in control of the universe and be a man at the same time), prayer (how He can respond to millions of people praying at the same moment), and foreknowledge (how He can know the future and we can still be free to choose whether to do something).

Summary

In this chapter Lewis wanted to deal with a difficulty some people have with the whole idea of prayer. How can God attend to "several hundred million" humans addressing Him at the same instant. Of course, the whole problem comes in the idea of "at the same moment." While our lives come to us instant by instant, it is not so for God. But time—past, present, and future—is not, as we take for granted that it is, the way things really exist. God is not *in* time at all. If millions of people pray to God at the same time, He need not listen to the "one little snippet" we call a particular moment in time. Every moment from the beginning of the world is always present for God.

How do you think of *time*? How does the dictionary define it? Should our view of sin and the Fall of mankind effect the notion of time?

This is a difficult concept to understand because we seem to have no referent point except time. But Lewis gave the example of writing a novel. If we are forced to stop writing for a moment because someone interrupts us, the imaginary time of the story has no interval. This is because we do not actually live in the imaginary world of the novel. While not a perfect illustration, it may give us a glance of the fact that God is not affected by the "Time-stream" of our physical universe." God does not live in a "Time-series" at all. For God Himself is life eternal.

When we understand both the notion of the Trinity and the idea that God is not restricted by time, then we see how much of what Christianity claims to be true can be true—the Incarnation, prayer, etc. While Jesus was on earth, the Father was still in heaven. While the Holy Spirit is in us, the Father and the Son are still in eternity.

There is yet another difficulty this idea—of God being outside of Time—helps to solve: This is the idea of God's knowing what we will do tomorrow, or divine foreknowledge, and our having free will. God can know what we will do tomorrow, and we can be free to choose to do it because God is not "trapped" in the time frame we are trapped in. He is "outside" and "above" our time line. What we call "tomorrow," God knows in just the same way as we know what we call "today."

 COMMENTARY

The central figure in history who expanded and defended the idea that God is not in time was Thomas Aquinas. True reality, not affected by the results of the Fall of man, is pictured as an Eternal Now by Aquinas. Time as we know it is the result of sin and decay. God is outside of time, outside of what we view as past, present, and future. God doesn't experience this "passage of instants." He is eternal in a true sense.

If we stop and think a bit, we can see an analogy—resemblance, parallel, similarity—of this *Eternal Now* in our fallen world. Human beings only experience the past in our memories and the future in our hopes and dreams. Even for us, it is always *now*; it is always the present. As you read this, it is now. Five seconds from now, if you are still reading, you will *think* of "now" as the past, but it will then be "now." Truly, the only real *experience* we have is of the "now." Well, the same is true of God, but He is outside, unaffected by, the limitations of our space-time universe. He is eternal, and His experience, naturally, would be of an Eternal Now, in contrast to the "temporal now" which we experience.

Incarnation—From the Latin *in*, "in," and *caro*, "flesh." In theology, this is the doctrine that God, the Eternal Son, the second person of the Trinity, became man, or flesh, in the person of Jesus. This does not mean, however, that He gave up His deity in the process (see John 1:14; Rom. 1:3; 8:3; Gal. 4:4; Phil. 2:7–8; 1 Tim. 3:16; Heb. 1; 1 John 4:2; 2 John 7)—Miethe, *The Compact Dictionary*, 114.

CHAPTER 4: GOOD INFECTION

Chapter at a Glance
This chapter explains that the love of God is eternal because He is an eternal being who has always experienced love between persons. The role of the Holy Spirit is explained.

Summary
Lewis wanted to try to explain how something can be the "source," "cause," or "origin" for another but not entail the one being there before the other. Now we have to look at the Trinity again. When we say that the Father, the first person of the Trinity, begot the Son, the second person; it does not mean that the Father was there before the Son, that the Father is eternal

Thomas Aquinas (1224/5–1274) was born in Northern Italy and taught two separate times at the University of Paris. The philosophy and theology based on his thought is known as *Thomism*. Aquinas taught that reason must support faith and that both reason and revelation prove the existence and nature of God. God is the Prime Mover, First Cause, Necessary and Supreme Being, the only self-existent Being, possessing no limitations, is changeless and unchangeable. Aquinas also taught that human beings possess free will given by God.

Aquinas built a system remarkable for its harmony and unity of thought. The fundamental principle of Thomism is the real distinction between an act and a potential act. By this principle is established the real distinction between essence and existence in created things, the truth of the principle of causality. His most famous writing was the *Summa Theologie*.

and the Son a little less so. The Son exists because the Father exists, but there never was a time before the Father produced the Son. With God as one being and three persons, no before or after is involved.

Lewis used the idea of two books. One book (call it "B") is lying on top of the other (call it "A") on a table, and this has always been the case. There never was a time when book A or book B did not exist. And both books have always been in that position. But clearly book B would not, could not, be in the position it is in if book A were not in the position it is in. In this sense, book A is causing the position of book B.

Think of the Son as always flowing forth from the Father, like light from a lamp, heat from a fire, thoughts from the mind. The Son is the "self-expression of the Father." And there never was a time when this was not so. But the pictures Lewis gave are also misleading because they seem to indicate that Father and Son are two separate things instead of two persons in one being. The Bible described the relationship with reference to "Father" and "Son" because this is better than any alternative we can come up with. Lewis thought it important for us to know that the relationship between these two persons is one of love: Father delights in Son; Son looks up to Father.

This is an important difference between Christianity and all other religions. In Christianity, God is no "static thing" but "a dynamic, pulsating activity, a life, almost a kind of drama. . . . The union between the Father and Son is such a live concrete thing that this union itself is also a Person. . . . What grows out of the joint life of the Father and Son is a real Person, is in fact the Third of the Three Persons who are God" (p. 152).

This third person of God is called the Holy Spirit. Lewis wrote that readers ought not be surprised if the Holy Spirit seems "more shadowy" in our minds. This is because usually in the Christian life we are not looking *at* Him because He is always acting through us. The Father is in front of us, so to speak, the Son beside us, and the Holy Spirit within us.

Being near God, in God, or having God in us is the "Good Infection." This comes as a result of letting God have His way. Thus, we come to share in the life of Christ. This is how we move from "bios," biological life, to "zoe," spiritual life. This is how we share in a life that was begotten, not made. This is how we come to eternal life because through Christ we are part of *the* Eternal Life. The Son came into this world so that He might infect humankind with the kind of life He is. The whole purpose of being a Christian is to become as He is.

COMMENTARY

Emerson is credited with having said: "Our families are people who know us but love us anyway." Well, whether this is true of our families, it is most certainly true of God! Lewis returned to the Trinity again. The statement that "God is love" can have no meaning unless God contains two "persons," unless there was the possibility in this one essence of sharing between persons. God wanted to share this love with us in sending part of Himself to love us and making it possible for the Him actually to become part of us. Because of God's ability

Holy Spirit—The third Person of the Trinity. The Holy Spirit is equal with the Father and Son (Matt. 28:19; 2 Cor. 13:14). Christians are reborn through the Holy Spirit (Acts 2:38). The Holy Spirit gave Christians gifts, such as the ability to speak in tongues, to prophesy, to heal and to work miracles (1 Cor. 12; 14). Jesus promised that when He departed, the Holy Spirit would come and dwell with every believer (John 14:16–26). He is called the Comforter, or Helper (John 14; 15:26; 16:7). He would guide and teach the church (John 15:25–26), bear witness to Christ and glorify Him (John 15:26), and convict the world of sin (John 16:7–14) and judgment (Luke 24:49; John 7:37–39; 14:25–26; Acts 1:8)—Miethe, *The Compact Dictionary*, 106–107.

Thank you, dear God, for the three greatest gifts you gave us mortals: being created in Your image with all the wonder that entails; salvation so truly undeserved; and that unbelievably satisfying, exceedingly joyful drink, a glass of clear cold water! Not only in the "sublime" do we have cause to be thankful but in every experience however small in which we give thanks to God for His goodness and in which we appreciate His creative power.

to love, He decided to give us a chance to be part of His eternal life. This infection of "zoe" brought by the Son was to restore us to what God intended us to be when He created us.

CHAPTER 5: THE OBSTINATE TOY SOLDIER

Chapter at a Glance

Natural man in his selfish desire is like an obstinate toy soldier who doesn't want to be turned into a real person and thus fights the transformation. But God, in sending His Son, made it possible for us to be real by becoming in one man what all men were intended to be.

Summary

God's Son became a man so that we could become children of God. The present state of things is that "zoe" and "bios" are not only different but also really opposed. Our natural life is self-centered. It wants to keep away from the "light and air" of "zoe," the spiritual world. Lewis likened this to people brought up dirty who are afraid of a bath. This makes sense in that our selfish "bios" knows that if "zoe" gets hold of us we will be changed, and we fight against this.

When we were children, most of us probably thought it would be fun if we could bring our toys to life. Lewis gave the example of a tin soldier who didn't like our trying to make him into flesh because he thought the "tin is being spoilt," that we were killing him. He would do everything to stop us from making him into a man if he could. Lewis didn't know what we would have done about the tin soldier, but he does know what God did about us.

The Son, second person of the godhead, became an actual fetus, a baby, and finally a man. We can perhaps get a picture of it if we think how we would like to become a "slug" or a "crab." But the result of God's becoming man was not only miraculous but also breathtaking.

How can we as Christians have victory over Satan in this life? How are Christian fellowship and the church important in this?

COMMENTARY

As Christians, we simply cannot afford to continue to cherish—nourish—any remnant of the "obstinate toy soldier" in us. When Satan has battered you mercilessly and all but beaten you and he thinks you are close to "throwing in the towel," he doesn't let up! He continually brings up old things, and anything he can, to try to push you over the edge, to try to defeat you totally. As contradictory as this may sound, when you are at your *weakest* you must be *strongest!* In such times, which try the depths of one's soul, you must especially turn to God for *His* strength and power. Only He can make you strong!

CHAPTER 6: TWO NOTES

Chapter at a Glance

This chapter is an attempt to avoid two misunderstandings which arose out of the last. The first is about why God didn't "*beget* many sons" if that is what He wanted, rather than "*make* 'toy soldiers.'"

Summary

To avoid misunderstanding, this chapter contains two notes which arise out of the last chapter.

1. A critic asked why God didn't *beget* many sons from the beginning instead of making "toy soldiers" who had to be brought to life by a

"difficult and painful process." Lewis said that one part of the answer is "fairly easy"; another part is likely beyond our ability to know. The easy part of the answer is that the process would not have been painful if the human race had not turned away from God so long ago as a result of free will. We are reminded that being able to love is much preferable to a "world of mere automata" who could never love.

With regard to why God didn't *beget* many sons, Lewis answered: Of course, all Christians believe there is only one Son of God. When referring to God, to ask if it could have been other than it is *is* "nonsensical." But, apart from this, Lewis argued that the very idea of the Father's "begetting" a number of sons from eternity is problematic: How would the supposed "many" sons be related to one another and to the Father? Perhaps nature itself was created exactly in order to make "many-ness" workable.

Totalitarian—The idea of an empire whose main characteristic is considered to be monolithic unity upheld by authoritarian means.

2. Individual differences and real individual people matter in Christianity. The idea of "one huge organism" with regard to humanity should not be confused with this fact. Christianity thinks of individual persons as "organs in a body," not as a simple list of items. As "organs," we are each different and contribute differently. God never intended us to be exactly alike; even our children should not be forced into our mold. On the other hand, every one of us experiences similar problems because we are part of the "same organism." A Christian must not be an individualist (forget we are all of the same organism) or a totalitarian (forget that each is a different organ).

COMMENTARY

Lewis wrote that real individual people matter in Christianity. His insight that, in Christ, a man or woman can truly become an individual, the very individual God intended him or her to be is most important. The world is full of carbon-copy wanna-bes who duplicate one another in the most despicable ways, even in the most terrible of sins. There is no question that something is terribly wrong with the values of the world. It is almost a "miracle" that the world is not even worse than it is. It is, after all (at least in the United States), living off of Christian moral capital to some degree, or it would be worse. When we see all the children killing children, all the school shootings, it begins to dawn on us just how morally bankrupt so many are!

CHAPTER 7: LET'S PRETEND

Chapter at a Glance

This chapter is about "pretending." At first we are pretending to be something we are not when we try to "dress up as Christ." A good kind of pretending leads to the real thing.

Summary

Two stories are put before us: First, "Beauty and the Beast." Second, a story about a man who had to wear a mask which make him look "nicer than he really was." In the first, the beast turns into a man, and "all went well." In the second, after years of wearing the mask, the man's face had grown to fit it, and he was now beautiful. Both stories, said Lewis, help illustrate what he wanted to say in this chapter, albeit in a fanciful way.

Why did God decide to create only two divine institutions: the family and the church? What is the practical significance of the fact that there are only two such institutions for a Christian?

There are two kinds of "pretending"—a bad kind (only the pretense is there instead of the real thing), and a good kind (when it leads to the real thing). Often the only way to get a particular quality is to start acting as if you have it already, as children do. When we start this good kind of pretending, soon we will see some ways we could actually make it more real.

In reality, it is not us, but God who does everything. At most, wrote Lewis, we allow it. In reality it is even God who does the pretending. He knows we are self-centered and greedy, but He says We will pretend this is "our Son," not a mere creature. God pretends in order to form the make-believe into a reality. Because of what the one true Son has done, the Father looks at us "as if " we are a "little Christ." Lewis knew this sounded "strange at first." But, is it? The "higher thing" always raises the lower; for example, the mother teaches the baby to talk by talking as if he knows the language "long before" he actually does.

 COMMENTARY

Once we have accepted Jesus as Savior and Lord, He works on us in many ways. Certainly, some ways are more direct and, therefore, should be more profitable, such as through the Bible, the church, and other Christians. This is why it is so important that we not forsake the "assembly of the saints"—the church. Some people who claim to be Christians don't see the value or importance of the church, but they are wrong. There are only two divinely created institutions: the family and the church. Both are important for believers!

CHAPTER 8: IS CHRISTIANITY HARD OR EASY?

Chapter at a Glance

At one and the same time, Christianity is both hard and easy. Jesus Himself spoke both ways. The Christian way is much easier than trying to do all we try to do as natural beings. But the hard part is seeing and being willing to surrender self to Him so that He may become part of us and us part of Him—that we may become Sons of God in Christ. This is the whole of Christianity.

Summary

"Putting on Christ" so that we can at last change into a "real son" is the whole of Christianity! Now we are told how this differs from "ordinary ideas" of ethics and "being good." The ordinary idea of morality is wrong because it says that we can somehow avoid doing wrong and do enough right that, in the end, our "poor natural self" will still have a chance to exist. It is like the honest man who pays taxes, hoping that after he does he will have enough to live.

In other words, we are still taking "our natural self" as the starting point. As long as we think this way, either we will give up the quest for goodness, or we will become unhappy. Make no mistake about it, said Lewis, as long as our natural self is in place, we will not have enough left to live on. With this starting point, in the end we will either give up trying to do good, or we will try to live "for others" in a "discontented, grubbing way." And this is worse than if you had "remained frankly selfish."

The real problem of the Christian life comes from the moment we awaken—in pushing back all our selfish goals and desires. When Jesus said

How many Christians today do you know personally who seem to be dedicating their lives to "putting on Christ." Why do you think that number is so small? Are we settling for mediocrity in our Christian living? What can individual Christians do to make Christlike living a priority? What can the church do?

The five most important decisions individuals have to make in life are: (1) belief in God and Christ Jesus, (2) to marry or not and whom, (3) their way to earn a living, (4) where and how they will live, and (5) whether to have children. Sadly many Christians make these important decisions by default or for the wrong reasons, or they allow others to make these decisions for them. Lewis believed that to use the energy of a lifetime to know and serve God is the most important thing a human being can do! How are you using the energy of your lifetime for God?

for us to "be perfect" (see Matt. 5:48), He was saying that "we must go in for the full treatment." Lewis reminded us that this is the whole of Christianity. It may look as if the church has a lot of objectives, but in reality it has only one—to draw all men to Christ. If any church is not doing that, it is simply wasting time. Not only did God become man for this purpose, but, Lewis said, the "whole universe" was created for the same purpose.

COMMENTARY

The real purpose of a Christian is not to torture our natural self but to put it to death! This will be a lifelong process. But the sooner we realize this and the sooner we begin trying to surrender self to God, the sooner we can start making wise decisions about how to use the energy of a lifetime.

CHAPTER 9: COUNTING THE COST

Chapter at a Glance
The process of being transformed into what God intended us to be when He created us is a long and painful one. It is not about just "improving" but about being perfected. Jesus warned us to count the costs before becoming Christians.

Summary
Some people were bothered by Lewis's words in the last chapter about becoming perfect. They interpreted his comments to mean that Christ would not help us unless we were perfect, and since this is not possible, our situation was hopeless. Lewis thought Christ meant that the only help He would give was to help us become perfect. He will give us nothing less than that *level* of help.

Lewis related this to his toothaches as a child. He knew that if he went to his mother she would give him medication to deaden the pain so he could sleep. But only when his pain was bad did he go because he knew the next morning meant going to the dentist. He couldn't get what he wanted without getting more than he wanted. And he knew the dentist wouldn't stop with examining that one tooth. When we go to Jesus to be cured of a particular sin, He will do it; but He will also give us the "full treatment."

Lewis said it is important to count the cost before we become Christians. Why is this important? What does it say about how the church's educational and evangelistic efforts should be structured?

Jesus warned people to "count the cost" before they become Christians. He is interested in nothing less than helping us be perfect if we allow Him to work in us. Yet the other side is that, even though Christ's goal is to help us reach perfection, He will be pleased with the "first feeble, stumbling effort" we make.

"God is easy to please, but hard to satisfy."—Gordon MacDonald

Lewis borrowed another parable from George MacDonald. We are asked to imagine ourselves as a house being rebuilt by God. At first we understand what is happening. The drains and the leaky roof are repaired. Then He starts major reconstruction. We thought we were going to be redesigned into a "decent little cottage," but God is "building a palace"—one He intends to come and live in Himself! The command to be perfect is neither idealistic nor unrealizable. The process is long and sometimes painful, but in the end He is going to build us into a "bright stainless mirror" which reflects back to God His goodness.

What kind of mirror are you? How do your life and actions reflect God?

 COMMENTARY

Though grace is the free gift of God, there is a cost to becoming a Christian, or should we say

there are expectations? Most believers do not know how to live the Christian life because they have only a minimal understanding of their faith. They try to live their entire lives on the first-grade level. They never engage in disciplined study. You simply cannot become a mature Christian by accident. In order to grow, you must discipline your life in study, prayer, worship, and fellowship. Besides pride or selfishness, the two greatest sins of Christians must be apathy and willful ignorance.

CHAPTER 10: NICE PEOPLE OR NEW MEN

Chapter at a Glance

Christianity calls us to be new people not simply nice people. Christians are works in progress, and this progress depends on our natural selves and our willingness to submit to God. While "niceness" is good and desirable, it is not really what the whole is about.

Summary

Jesus meant what He said. By putting ourselves in His hands, we will be perfected; but this rebuilding process will not be completed in this lifetime. Death itself is an important part of the treatment. Lewis turned to an often-asked question: Why aren't all Christians "obviously nicer" people than unbelievers if all this Christian stuff is true? Behind the question we find a reasonable and an unreasonable part.

First, the reasonable part: If conversion makes no difference in a person's outward actions, then we must be suspicious that it was "largely imaginary." "Fine feelings, new insights" mean nothing unless our actual behavior is changed for the better. In one sense the "outer world" is right to judge Christianity by results. Trees *are* known by their fruit!

God regards a "nasty nature" as a grievous thing. But, in an important sense, "niceness" is not the point at all. What God wants—has been watching, waiting, working for—is something only an individual can give God—the self, one's own nature. God can help, but He will not force anyone to yield.

Why is it so much more important that we be concerned with being *new* people rather than *nice* people?

A paradox must be noted here: Actually, even a person's niceness is a gift *from* God, not that person's gift *to* God. But unless a person bends in the direction of God, he will think the "niceness" is his own. And as long as he thinks in this way, the niceness is definitely *not* his own! Only when we realize that the particular virtue is not ours at all but God's gift to us and only when we offer it back to God does it begin to be ours in any meaningful sense. This is how we begin to partake in our own creation.

Here we find a "warning or an encouragement" for each of us. First, the warning is clear: "If you are a nice—virtuous—person beware! God expects much from those to whom much has been given. If we mistake what are really God's gifts to us through nature as our own merits, and we are contented so, we are still in a state of rebellion. We must remember that Satan was once an archangel with high natural gifts. Look where they got him!

Now the encouragement: If you are a "poor creature," "saddled" with a disgusting sexual perversion, pestered almost constantly with an inferiority complex, don't despair! Christ not only knows about all this, but you are also "one of the poor" He blessed (Matt. 5:3). Christ knows what a "wretched machine" we are attempting to

81

drive. Keep on trying! One day He will put this one "on the scrap-heap" and give a new one which will be fitted for eternity.

In the whole universe there is only one soul we really know and only one whose fate is truly in our hands. We cannot justifiably put God off because of conjectures about our neighbors. None of this nonsense matters one whit in the real "Presence" in which we now stand, nor will it when we stand face-to-face and He cannot be denied.

COMMENTARY

We aren't called to be nice people but new people. And yet we should expect Christians to be improving. Often the problem with the church, or individuals, is not that they do not witness. Fortunately or unfortunately, we are always witnessing—to what we are and to what we are not, to what we should be and aren't, or to what we should be and are! And people outside the church clearly see this witness, positive or negative. Public proclamation, whether from a pulpit or in personal witnessing, is never convincing unless it is perceived as true of the life lived.

Remember the old bumper sticker: "Be patient with me; God isn't finished with me yet." What does it mean to be an *improving* Christian? How can you work at this in your church, family, and as an individual? Why did Lewis say it was important to try to improve?

CHAPTER 11: THE NEW MEN

Chapter at a Glance
In the Christian view, the New Man appeared two thousand years ago. This New Step not only came from outside nature but differs in several other ways.

Summary
Jesus means to transform us, not just improve us. The nearest comparison in our world, Lewis declared, is discovered in the "remarkable transformations" in insects. We may be better able to

understand the Christian idea with reference to evolution. "Thousands of centuries" in the past "huge, very heavily armoured creatures" existed. If we had been observing the process then, we would have expected more and heavier armor in the future. But instead we got "little, naked, unarmoured animals" with "better brains." The next step was more than just different. It had a "new kind of difference," one quite unexpected.

The transformation into new creations of God can be compared to this. The difference will be a new kind of difference—not just change, but a new way of producing change. This new step will not be a "stage of Evolution" in any case. In fact, in the Christian view the Next Step has already come into view. It is not a change of "brainy" to "brainier." It is a change from being creatures God created to being His sons. Jesus, of course, is the first example. This is why the change is not from nature but from outside of nature.

 COMMENTARY

Again, we are called to remember that the issue is transformation. It would be good here to recall the Christian doctrine of repentance (see: *Shepherd's Notes* for chapter 4, Book II). Yes, this transformation into a new creation looks, if one takes the example of evolution, to be of a "new kind," but this is a good example of where Lewis missed the boat, missed an opportunity in a way. This "new kind," this "zoe," is actually the *original* kind—reality as it was originally and as it was meant to be.

Christianity is always just one generation away from extinction. How have you "changed" by becoming a Christian? How will you ensure that the next generation knows about Jesus Christ?

BIBLIOGRAPHY

Barratt, David. *C. S. Lewis and His World*. Grand Rapids: Eerdmans, 1987.

Christensen, Michael. *C. S. Lewis on Scripture*. Waco, TX: Word, 1979; London: Hodder, 1980.

Christopher, Joe R. and Joan K. Ostling. *C. S. Lewis: An Annotated Checklist of Writings about Him and His Works*. Kent, OH: Kent State University Press, 1974.

Como, James T. (ed.). *C. S. Lewis at the Breakfast Table: And Other Reminiscences*. New York: Macmillan, 1979.

Cunningham, Richard B. *C. S. Lewis: Defender of the Faith*. Philadelphia: Westminster Press, 1967.

Gibson, Evan. *C. S. Lewis, Spinner of Tales*. Grand Rapids: Eerdmans, 1980.

Gilbert, Douglas and Clyde Kilby. *C. S. Lewis: Images of His World*. Grand Rapids: Eerdmans, 1973.

Green, Michael. *Runaway World*. Downers Grove, IL.: Intervarsity Press, 1968.

Gresham, Douglas H. *Lenten Lands: My Childhood with Joy Davidman and C. S. Lewis*. New York: Macmillan, 1988.

Howard, Thomas. *The Achievement of C. S. Lewis*. Wheaton, IL.: Harold Shaw, 1980.

Keefe, Carolyn. *C. S. Lewis: Speaker and Teacher*. Grand Rapids: Zondervan, 1971.

Kilby, Clyde. *Images of Salvation in the Fiction of C. S. Lewis*. Wheaton, IL.: Harold Shaw, 1978.

_____. *The Christian World of C. S. Lewis*. Grand Rapids: Eerdmans, 1964.

Kreeft, Peter. *C. S. Lewis: A Critical Essay*. Grand Rapids: Eerdmans, 1969.

Lindskoog, Kathryn. *The C. S. Lewis Hoax*. Portland, OR.: Multnomah Press, 1988.

Miethe, Terry L. *The Compact Dictionary of Doctrinal Terms*. Minneapolis, MN.: Bethany House, 1988.

Peters, John. *C. S. Lewis: The Man and his Achievement*. London: Paternoster, 1985.

Purtill, Richard. *Lord of the Elves and Eldils: Fantasy and Philosophy in C. S. Lewis and J. R. R. Tolkien*. Grand Rapids: Zondervan, 1974.

Sayer, George. *Jack: A Life of C. S. Lewis*. Wheaton, IL.: Crossway Books, 1994.

Schakel, Peter, Jr. (ed.). *The Longing for a Form: Essays on the Fiction of C. S. Lewis*. Kent, OH: Kent State University Press, 1977.

Sibley, Brian. *Shadowlands*. London: Hodder & Stoughton, 1985.

Walsh, Chad. *C. S. Lewis: Apostle to the Skeptics*. New York: Macmillan, 1949; Folcraft, PA.: Folcraft Library Editions, 1974.

_____. *The Literary Legacy of C. S. Lewis*. New York: Harcourt Brace Jovanovich, 1980.